CONSTITUTIONAL
AMENDMENTS
BEYOND THE BILL OF RIGHTS

Amendment XVII
Establishing Election
to the U.S. Senate

Other Books of Related Interest

Opposing Viewpoints Series

American Values

Civil Liberties

Political Campaigns

The U.S. Supreme Court

Current Controversies Series

Federal Elections

The U.S. Economy

CONSTITUTIONAL
AMENDMENTS
BEYOND THE BILL OF RIGHTS

Amendment XVII
Establishing Election
to the U.S. Senate

Jeff Hay, Book Editor

GREENHAVEN PRESS
A part of Gale, Cengage Learning

GALE
CENGAGE Learning™

Detroit • New York • San Francisco • New Haven, Conn • Waterville, Maine • London

Christine Nasso, *Publisher*
Elizabeth Des Chenes, *Managing Editor*

© 2010 Greenhaven Press, a part of Gale, Cengage Learning.

Gale and Greenhaven Press are registered trademarks used herein under license.

For more information, contact:
Greenhaven Press
27500 Drake Rd.
Farmington Hills, MI 48331-3535
Or you can visit our Internet site at gale.cengage.com

For product information and technology assistance, contact us at

Gale Customer Support, 1-800-877-4253
For permission to use material from this text or product, submit all requests online at
www.cengage.com/permissions

Further permissions questions can be emailed to permissionrequest@cengage.com

Articles in Greenhaven Press anthologies are often edited for length to meet page requirements. In addition, original titles of these works are changed to clearly present the main thesis and to explicitly indicate the author's opinion. Every effort is made to ensure that Greenhaven Press accurately reflects the original intent of the authors. Every effort has been made to trace the owners of copyrighted material.

Cover photograph © Ralf-Finn Hestoft/Corbis.

LIBRARY OF CONGRESS CATALOGING-IN-PUBLICATION DATA

Amendment XVII : establishing election to the U.S. Senate / Jeff Hay, book editor.
    p. cm. -- (Constitutional amendments: beyond the Bill of Rights)
    Includes bibliographical references and index.
    ISBN 978-0-7377-4697-6 (hardcover) -- ISBN 978-0-7377-5112-3 (pbk.)
    1. United States. Senate--Elections. 2. Election law--United States. 3. United States. Constitution. 17th Amendment--History. I. Hay, Jeff. II. Title: Amendment 17. III. Title: Amendment seventeen. IV. Title: Establishing election to the U.S. Senate.
    KF4913.A954 2010
    342.73'055--dc22

                                                2009054110

Printed in the United States of America
1 2 3 4 5 6 7 14 13 12 11 10

Contents

Chapter 1: Historical Background on the Seventeenth Amendment

A. Maurice Low

The author of an article published ten years before the appearance of the Seventeenth Amendment argues that, not only does the Senate dominate the House of Representatives and often even the president, but an even smaller group of long-standing senators wields the true power within the U.S. government.

David Graham Phillips

Focusing on the career of Maryland senator Arthur P. Gorman, a "muckraking" journalist in 1906 describes the Senate as the arm of major industries seeking government privileges.

Lewis L. Gould

Elections in 1910 resulted in a Democratic majority in Congress for the first time in many years. Among the measures they energetically undertook was a constitutional amendment to give ordinary citizens the chance to elect senators directly.

The New York Times

Debates on the proposed Seventeenth Amendment grew heated in the U.S. Senate, with some members rejecting a proposal that the national government set election rules for senators in individual states. They feared that it might empower African American voters.

Chapter 2: Calls to Repeal or Change the Seventeenth Amendment

Federalism is the tradition in America whereby the states should have distinct identities and freedoms of their own as part of a larger federal union. In a statement made during his last year in office, former Georgia senator Zell Miller argues that the Seventeenth Amendment helped end that tradition.

Even though the corrupt actions of former Illinois governor Rod Blagojevich in appointing a senator to replace Barack Obama brought the Seventeenth Amendment into question, returning to a system in which state legislators choose senators is not the answer. Direct democracy is always preferable.

Chapter 3: The Seventeenth Amendment in Contemporary America

Following the 2008 elections, many states had to replace senators headed to the presidency, the vice presidency, and several cabinet posts. This cluster of replacements shed light on the various state laws and practices that, in most cases, allow governors to choose replacements until the next election cycle. This stands in contrast with the House of Representatives, where replacements are chosen in special elections.

An ailing Senator Edward Kennedy of Massachusetts, one of the Senate's longest-serving members, wanted the Massachusetts state government to be able to replace him quickly when and if he became unable to continue serving.

Appendix

Establishing Election
to the U.S. Senate

> *"Today's Constitution is a realistic docu-
> ment of freedom only because of several
> corrective amendments. Those amend-
> ments speak to a sense of decency and
> fairness."*
>
> *Thurgood Marshall*

While the U.S. Constitution forms the backbone of American democracy, the amendments make the Constitution a living, ever-evolving document. Interpretation and analysis of the Constitution inform lively debate in every branch of government, as well as among students, scholars, and all other citizens, and views on various articles of the Constitution have changed over the generations. Formally altering the Constitution, however, can happen only through the amendment process. The Greenhaven Press series The Bill of Rights examines the first ten amendments to the Constitution. Constitutional Amendments: Beyond the Bill of Rights continues the exploration, addressing key amendments ratified since 1791.

The process of amending the Constitution is painstaking. While other options are available, the method used for nearly every amendment begins with a congressional bill that must pass both the Senate and the House of Representatives by a two-thirds majority. Then the amendment must be ratified by three-quarters of the states. Many amendments have been proposed since the Bill of Rights was adopted in 1791, but only seventeen have been ratified.

It may be difficult to imagine a United States where women and African Americans are prohibited from voting, where the federal government allows one human being to enslave another, or where some citizens are denied equal protection under the law. While many of our most fundamental liberties are protected by the Bill of Rights, the amendments that followed have significantly broadened and enhanced the rights of American citizens. Such rights may be taken for granted today, but when the amendments were ratified, many were considered groundbreaking and proved to be explosively controversial.

Each volume in Constitutional Amendments provides an in-depth exploration of an amendment and its impact through primary and secondary sources, both historical and contemporary. Primary sources include landmark Supreme Court rulings, speeches by prominent experts, and newspaper editorials. Secondary sources include historical analyses, law journal articles, book excerpts, and magazine articles. Each volume first presents the historical background of the amendment, creating a colorful picture of the circumstances surrounding the amendment's passage: the campaigns to sway public opinion, the congressional debates, and the struggle for ratification. Next, each volume examines the ways the court system has been used to test the validity of the amendment and addresses the ramifications of the amendment's passage. The final chapter of each volume presents viewpoints that explore current controversies and debates relating to ways in which the amendment affects our everyday lives.

Numerous features are included in each Constitutional Amendments volume:

- An originally written introduction presents a concise yet thorough overview of the amendment.

- A time line provides historical context by describing key events, organizations, and people relating to the ratification of the amendment, subsequent court cases, and the impact of the amendment.

- An annotated table of contents offers an at-a-glance summary of each primary and secondary source essay included in the volume.

- The complete text of the amendment, followed by a "plain English" explanation, brings the amendment into clear focus for students and other readers.

- Graphs, charts, tables, and maps enhance the text.

- A list of all twenty-seven Constitutional Amendments offers quick reference.

- An annotated list of court cases relevant to the amendment broadens the reader's understanding of the judiciary's role in interpreting the Constitution.

- A bibliography of books, periodicals, and Web sites aids readers in further research.

- A detailed subject index allows readers to quickly find the information they need.

With the aid of this series, students and other researchers will become better informed of their rights and responsibilities as American citizens. Constitutional Amendments: Beyond the Bill of Rights examines the roots of American democracy, bringing to life the ways the Constitution has evolved and how it has impacted this nation's history.

Amendment Text and Explanation

The Seventeenth Amendment to the United States Constitution

Passed by Congress May 13, 1912. Ratified April 8, 1913.

Note: Article I, section 3, of the Constitution was modified by the Seventeenth Amendment.

The Senate of the United States shall be composed of two Senators from each State, elected by the people thereof, for six years; and each Senator shall have one vote. The electors in each State shall have the qualifications requisite for electors of the most numerous branch of the State legislatures.

When vacancies happen in the representation of any State in the Senate, the executive authority of such State shall issue writs of election to fill such vacancies: Provided, That the legislature of any State may empower the executive thereof to make temporary appointments until the people fill the vacancies by election as the legislature may direct.

This amendment shall not be so construed as to affect the election or term of any Senator chosen before it becomes valid as part of the Constitution.

Explanation

The first paragraph of the Seventeenth Amendment reiterates the principles originally stated in the U.S. Constitution, that each individual state will have two senators representing it in the federal government. Each of these two senators will serve for terms of six years, and, in the key modification represented by the Seventeenth Amendment, those senators will be elected by the people of the state from which they come. The first paragraph concludes by asserting that voters in senatorial races must have the same qualifications for voting as those who cast their ballots for representatives in the legislatures of the individual states.

The second paragraph of the Seventeenth Amendment is concerned with the issue of senatorial replacements; in other words, what states should do if a sitting senator resigns, passes away, or moves on to another office. In general, the governors of states were granted the right to plan for new elections to choose senatorial replacements, maintaining the key Seventeenth Amendment principle that senators should be chosen by the people. But states were also given the ability to provide governors with the right to appoint replacements until these elections could be held. This was done to ensure that each state would be able to maintain its full complement of two senators even in the months (or sometimes years) before new elections took place.

The final portion of the Seventeenth Amendment assures that any senator in office would not be affected by the amendment until it was duly ratified and became part of the Constitution.

Introduction

In the 2008 presidential election a sitting senator, Barack Obama of Illinois, was elected as the forty-fourth president of the United States. Obama chose as his running mate another sitting senator, Joe Biden of Delaware. Soon after the election, when Obama selected his cabinet, other active senators found themselves about to change jobs; namely, Hillary Rodham Clinton of New York, who became Obama's new secretary of state, and Ken Salazar of Colorado, the new secretary of the interior.

The composition of the United States Senate was about to undergo major shifts as these four members had to be replaced at the same time as a number of new senators took office, having been elected in November 2008. Indeed, the transformation continued well into 2009 with one new senator, Al Franken of Minnesota, seated only in July following a very close contest and a series of court battles. Meanwhile one of the Senate's longest-serving members, Edward M. Kennedy of Massachusetts, died in late August, necessitating yet another replacement.

The issues of senatorial elections and replacements have been contentious ones in American history. The Senate is the "upper" house of the U.S. Congress, the American version of the British House of Lords and named for the council of elders, or "senate," of the ancient Roman Republic. And while membership in the Senate is by no means hereditary, as it is in the House of Lords, the body maintains a status in American political culture that is as close as the United States gets to aristocracy. Senators are elected for terms of six years, longer even than the presidential four-year term, and for some, like Edward Kennedy, the job becomes a virtually permanent one because their constituents keep sending them back. A senator for forty-seven years, Kennedy shared much of that time with other senators who were reelected repeatedly, such as Ted Stevens of Alaska, who was in the Senate from 1968 to 2009. Meanwhile, the Senate maintains certain privileges not accorded to its counterpart, the "lower" House of Representatives. These include the ability to approve or disapprove of presidential appointments to the cabinet and Supreme Court as well as to approve or disapprove of foreign treaties. Adding to the Senate's prestige are the facts that there are only one hundred members, two from each of the fifty states, and that these officials serve comparatively large constituencies. For much of U.S. history, indeed, senators have been the most vocal defenders of the rights of the states with regard to states' relationships with the national government. With such responsibilities and so much status granted to the Senate, it is no surprise that the ways its members are chosen have been controversial.

When the American republic was founded in the 1780s and the U.S. Constitution written, leaders decided that senators would be chosen by the legislatures of the individual states rather than by voters. This was a reflection of the belief, prominent at the time, that individual states needed to maintain a political sovereignty and legal identity separate from that of the national government. Legislatures, acting in the interests of their states, would choose senators who would also pursue states' interests even while being prominent leaders at the national level. Putting the choice of senators in the hands of legislatures, it was thought, would leave those chosen free from having to worry about seeking votes in general elections, a burden that six-year terms further freed them from. Indeed, it would be members of the House of Representatives, the "people's" house, who would be directly elected by the voting population. Because these House members served terms of only two years, they needed to go back to the voters often and were on the whole considered the true representatives of the people at the national level. The selection of senators by state legislatures resulted in the emergence of such senatorial pow-erhouses as Daniel Webster of Massachusetts, Henry Clay of Kentucky, and John C. Calhoun of South Carolina, all of whom were more respected and influential than some of the presidents they served in the decades prior to the American Civil War (1861–65).

Legislative selection of senators, however, was not without its problems. States maintained a variety of procedures for ac-tually making their choices, and sometimes the procedures were unclear enough that they could be challenged in court, thus delaying the selection and seating of a senator for months or even years. In some instances, senators "bought" their of-fices by bribing members of state legislatures or, more subtly, found ways to influence their votes by bringing economic or political pressure to bear. Examples include William Lorimer, who, through intermediaries unknown to him, was elected to the Senate in 1909 only after some of those who voted for him were bribed.

By the end of the 1800s, senators faced increasing accusa-tions that they represented factions within states, rather than states themselves, or even very narrow economic interests such as large corporations. Critics also decried the "Lorimerism" that allowed for bribery and corruption. Calls grew louder to attack these problems by making the Senate less elite and aris-tocratic in tone and more responsive to the people senators were supposed to represent. The Seventeenth Amendment emerged out of these calls for reform.

The Seventeenth Amendment, which provided for direct election of senators by voters rather than by state legislatures, is generally credited to the Progressive Movement in American politics in the first two decades of the twentieth century. But the calls for direct election of senators began long before. As far back as 1828, incoming president Andrew Jackson had called for the direct election of senators, while in the 1870s, the state of Nebraska began the use of primaries. In these, party candidates for the Senate were chosen by popular vote, although the actual selection remained with the state legislature. By the first decades of the 1900s more than twenty additional states had begun to use primaries. Oregon, by 1907, had gone so far as to shift to direct elections entirely, and Nebraska followed suit soon after. These reforms took place in the face of much opposition from the Senate itself, particularly a core of "old guard" senators in the Republican Party. These longtimers, claiming the need to preserve the Senate's privileges and status, blocked five attempts between 1893 and 1910 to introduce a constitutional amendment calling for direct election of senators.

The Progressives, for their part, pursued a wide variety of political, economic, and social changes in the first part of the twentieth century. Their efforts included America's first environmental legislation; the breaking up of powerful industrial monopolies, or trusts; and the passage of the Nineteenth Amendment, which gave women the right to vote. They maintained a strong interest in the rights of ordinary people relative to those of powerful institutions, so it was no surprise they would support moves to require direct election of senators.

The progressive case for reform was strengthened by a group of "muckraking" journalists who sought to expose in print the excesses and corruption of such institutions as large corporations and even the U.S. Senate. Many of these so-called muckrakers worked for publications owned by the outspoken multimillionaire William Randolph Hearst, who saw muckraking as a way both to expose abuses and to make money by selling advertisements, newspapers, and magazines. In 1906 the Hearst muckraker David Graham Phillips published a series of articles in *Cosmopolitan* magazine titled The Treason of the Senate. It described the Senate as a body dominated by a small group of prominent members who saw their main responsibility as serving their economic and industrial allies rather than the needs of their states and constituents. Phillips went so far as to name those senators he saw as most beholden to special interests. Other muckrakers, meanwhile, decried the elitist nature of the Senate as it then stood, calling it more powerful even than presidents.

In this atmosphere of change and reform, the momentum grew for a new constitutional amendment to require direct election of senators. In 1911 Senator Joseph Bristow of Kansas introduced such an amendment. It enjoyed a great deal of support, often from newcomers to the Senate whose elections were the result of the recent moves in many states toward primaries or direct elections. But it was also strongly opposed and the source of months of debate. Among those who objected most loudly to Bristow's proposal were senators from southern and near-southern states (such as Maryland) who had two related concerns. One was that any new amendment would be an unjustified interference in state affairs on the part of the federal government. The other was that the federal government might use the new measure to guarantee the voting rights of African Americans. Nonetheless, Bristow's proposed amendment was approved by the Senate, with some changes. It was also approved by the House of Representatives and then sent on to the states for ratification. By April of 1913 it had been ratified by thirty-six of the forty-eight states, the three-quarters constitutionally necessary, and Bristow's modified proposal became the Seventeenth Amendment to the U.S. Constitution. Eleven states remain on record as having either rejected or not ratified the amendment.

The Seventeenth Amendment, in comparison with many of the other constitutional amendments, has remained fairly uncontroversial. There have been some who have claimed, like Senate historian George Haynes, that the amendment has made the Senate less effective by reducing its level of prestige and making members raise funds for elections as well as having to seek votes. But for most of the decades since its ratification there have been few calls for its repeal; neither has it been at the center of major court cases, including those heard by the U.S. Supreme Court. Few people, it seems, are willing to challenge the principle of direct elections, and the Senate itself has done a reasonable job of maintaining its status as an elite representative body.

Only in the years since 2000 has the Seventeenth Amendment been the source of new controversy and calls for repeal. One charge, stated vocally by former Georgia senator Zell Miller in 2004, was that the need to take part in America's increasingly expensive elections made senators, or would-be senators, spend a great deal of time raising money. The need for funds also makes senators dependent on those, whether corporations, individuals, or other organizations, who provide the money for election campaigns. Miller, whose opinions were seconded by other conservative voices, felt that a repeal of the Seventeenth Amendment would also strengthen America's federalism in an age when, he argued, the national government was growing too powerful at the expense of the states. Miller's formal proposal for repeal, despite the supporting voices, did not last long in the Senate.

The issue of senatorial replacements, not direct election of senators, has been the main source of controversy in recent years. Sitting senators might resign, take on new jobs, or pass away and therefore require replacements. The language of the Seventeenth Amendment provides that in such cases state governors can choose temporary replacements but that ultimately general elections should be held to replace senators. States have interpreted this language in various ways. In general, some states hold that any temporary senators only hold their seats until a special election can be held, and indeed, replacements in the House of Representatives are always the product of special elections. Other states have followed a practice of allowing gubernatorial appointments to remain in the Senate until the next round of general elections. Because senators serve such long terms, this might mean that for a number of years a state might have a senator who not only is not elected by the voters but is not even chosen by a state legislature. Instead, he or she was appointed by a governor.

Examples of both alternatives appeared following the general elections and senatorial shakeups of 2008. In Illinois, Governor Rod Blagojevich selected a replacement for President-elect Obama. But Blagojevich was soon accused of offering the office to a buyer in exchange for political favors, bringing to mind some of the examples of Lorimerism that had inspired the Seventeenth Amendment in the first place. The allegations were serious enough that Blagojevich was impeached, although his choice for the Senate, Roland Burris, was ultimately cleared and allowed to remain in his seat until the 2010 elections.

The possibility of gubernatorial appointments opening the door to not only influence peddling but also dynasty building appeared in other states as well. The initial frontrunner to take Hillary Rodham Clinton's place in New York was Caroline Kennedy, the daughter of a former president and niece of a current senator, who had no political experience. Kennedy eventually took herself out of the running. Biden's replacement in Delaware, his former chief of staff, was accused of being no more than a placeholder until Biden's son Beau could be elected, while in Colorado, Ken Salazar's brother, Representative John Salazar, was considered a candidate until another official was ultimately chosen.

All four of these replacements were selected by their state's governors, the procedure that was settled on as a compromise when the Seventeenth Amendment's terms were initially being negotiated. Having governors choose replacements was, and is, thought to be a useful procedure because those chosen can be seated quickly, ensuring that each state maintains its full complement of two senators. The dangers of such gubernatorial selections, such as influence peddling or nepotism, would be lessened by the fact that any senatorial replacement would ultimately face election or leave office—indeed, a number of such replacements have made it clear that they only planned to serve out the terms of their predecessors.

Controversies have arisen, however, over the timing of these elections. In most states, procedures call for replacement senators to remain in office until the next round of general elections. Roland Burris in Illinois, for example, would stay in the seat originally won by Obama until 2010. While this involves only a two-year term, other appointed senatorial replacements might find themselves in office for four or five years before the next round of general elections, opening the door to charges that these replacement senators were not elected by the people and are not merely holding the seat until they can be elected. An alternative would be to hold a special election, as is the procedure in every state to choose replacements for U.S. representatives.

Such a controversy appeared following the death of Senator Edward Kennedy of Massachusetts in August 2009. Kennedy's death, and his potential replacement, marked the end of a long political dynasty and was therefore the focus of much attention. Massachusetts law, unlike that of most states, requires a special election to be held 145 to 160 days after a Senate seat opens up, but that law is a relatively new one. It was passed in 2004 when the possibility existed that Kennedy's counterpart, Senator John Kerry, might be elected president. The state's mostly Democratic legislature did not want to leave the choice of a replacement in the hands of then-governor Mitt Romney, a Republican. Now, however, and at the urging of Kennedy himself, dying of cancer, state officials planned to change the law so that, once again, the governor could appoint a replacement, at least until the special election could be held. In late September 2009, both the House and Senate of Massachusetts approved the new law, and Democratic governor Deval Patrick appointed Paul Kirk to be

Kennedy's replacement. A special election was scheduled for January 2010, by which time sympathy for Kennedy had been replaced by dissatisfaction with Obama's Democratic presidency, resulting in the election of Scott Brown, a Republican, over the seeming shoo-in, Democrat Martha Coakley.

Chronology

1775–1783

The American Revolution is fought by thirteen British colonies strung along the Atlantic Coast of North America. The colonies successfully break away from Britain to form the United States of America.

1787

A constitutional convention meets in Philadelphia to begin drafting a constitution by which the United States of America will be governed. The draft is finished by the end of the year. Among its proposals is that the upper house of the U.S. government would be a body known as the Senate. Each individual state would choose two senators who would serve terms of six years. The two would be chosen by each state's legislature.

1788

The Constitution is ratified by the required nine of the original thirteen states. The last of the nine to ratify is Virginia, which proposes to add to it a Bill of Rights.

1791

Congress adds the first ten amendments to the Constitution as the Bill of Rights.

1828

Andrew Jackson, who advocated changing the Constitution to allow for the direct election of senators, is elected president.

1866

The U.S. Congress passes a law attempting to regulate the ways state legislatures choose senators.

1870s

The state of Nebraska begins to hold primaries in which candidates for the Senate are chosen by popular election, although the state legislature retained the final choice. Other states follow.

1892

A constitutional amendment calling for the direct election of senators is first introduced. Similar proposals were made every year thereafter for more than a decade.

1906

Muckraking journalist David Graham Phillips publishes a four-part series of articles called The Treason of the Senate. It accuses the Senate of being corrupted by financial and business interests.

The state of Oregon chooses on its own to hold direct elections for senators.

1909

Senator William Lorimer of Illinois is accused of paying a state legislator to help vote him into office. The incident spurs widespread calls for a new amendment installing direct elections of senators.

1910

Elections sweep a number of so-called progressives into the U.S. Congress. Many of them are open to reforms such as the direct election of senators.

1911

Senator Joseph L. Bristow of Kansas introduces a seventeenth constitutional amendment in the Senate.

1912

Following tense negotiations over such issues as congressional interference into state election procedures, the proposed Seventeenth Amendment is approved by both the Senate and House of Representatives. It is then sent on to the states for ratification.

1913

On April 8, Connecticut becomes the thirty-sixth state to ratify the Seventeenth Amendment. Having thus garnered the three-quarters of the then forty-eight states necessary for ratification, the Seventeenth Amendment is added to the U.S. Constitution. Louisiana also subsequently ratified the amendment.

1959

Alaska and Hawaii are added to the union as the forty-ninth and fiftieth states, respectively. They accepted the Constitution as it stood, including the Seventeenth Amendment, making the total of ratifying states thirty-nine.

2003

The State Judiciary Committee in Montana approves a measure calling for the repeal of the Seventeenth Amendment, but it dies in the state senate.

2004

Senator Zell Miller of Georgia, himself a senatorial replacement chosen by his state's governor in 1999 and then confirmed via special election, calls for a new constitutional amendment repealing the Seventeenth Amendment.

2005

Senators Russ Feingold of Wisconsin and John McCain of Arizona, along with Representative David Dreier of California, call for a new amendment ending the ability of governors to choose senatorial replacements.

2008–2009

The issue of senatorial replacements receives new attention as Illinois senator Barack Obama and Delaware senator Joseph Biden are elected president and vice president, respectively.

CONSTITUTIONAL
AMENDMENTS
BEYOND THE BILL OF RIGHTS

CHAPTER 1

Historical Background on the Seventeenth Amendment

The Senate Is the Real Power in the U.S. Government

A. Maurice Low

One of the inspirations for the Seventeenth Amendment was a perception among some elected officials and government observers that the Senate had grown too powerful and influential, that it was an exclusive and elitist club that did not truly represent the American people. In the following selection from an article published in 1901, journalist A. Maurice Low makes this argument. He argues that the power of the Senate is more a matter of custom, tradition, and political etiquette than of written statute but that this power is very real nevertheless. Senators, he claims, can always prevent legislation from being passed if they are determined enough, even if the majority of the Congress favors it. Senators can even get in the way of presidents, who must cultivate a careful relationship with the representative body if they hope to succeed. Low also notes that status within the Senate itself is dependent upon seniority and that those senators who serve long enough to rise to leadership positions in important committees wield a great deal of power. A. Maurice Low wrote articles on American and world affairs as well as on Washington, D.C., society for many magazines, such as Harper's, *in the first three decades of the twentieth century. His books include* Woodrow Wilson: An Interpretation.

Over the doors of the Senate of the United States might well be inscribed the motto, *"Do ut des,"* for it expresses the principle which governs the members of the Senate, especially the inner circle that really controls the Upper House of Congress, that is, in fact, the government of the United States. [German leader from 1871 to 1890 Otto von] Bismarck trans-

A. Maurice Low, "The Oligarchy of the Senate," *The North American Review*, vol. 54, 1901–1902.

lated this maxim and used it in the sense of "I give in order that you may give;" [British politician George] Goschen rendered it into English as "the exchange of friendly offices, based on the avowed self-interest of the parties." Whether the Bismarckian or the Goschen version be accepted, the result is the same.

The founders of the Republic, while creating all possible precautions against the usurpation of the Executive, could not altogether close their eyes to the dangers which might come from legislative assumptions. [U.S. founding father James] Madison wrote that the founders of the Republic "seem never to have recollected the danger from legislative usurpations, which, by assembling all power in the same hands, must lead to the same tyranny as is threatened by executive usurpations." And again: "It is against the enterprising ambition of this department [the legislative] that the people ought to indulge all their jealousy and exhaust all their precautions." [Founding father Alexander] Hamilton pointed this warning: "The tendency of the legislative authority to absorb every other has been fully displayed and illustrated by example in some preceding number. . . . The representatives of the people . . . often appear disposed to exert an imperious control over the other departments." . . .

The Senate and the House

Basing the Federal Constitution on the British system, *mutatis mutandis* [changing what was necessary], the framers of the Constitution might well regard the House as having higher authority than the Senate, because it had the sole power to originate money bills. While that is technically correct, the power of the Senate over money bills is, in some respects, even greater than that of the House, since it is able to amend any bill which the House may send to it for concurrent action. This was the very thing feared by [founding father George] Mason, of Virginia, and pointed out by him; and the right of the Senate to originate, by the power of amendment, bills raising revenue and making appropriations has been confirmed by judicial approval. Technically, such bills have not originated, or rather have not been initiated, in the Senate. But when the Senate takes, for example, a tariff bill, strikes out all except the enacting clause, writes in and returns to the House a new bill, which that body is compelled to accept, it may be asked whether that particular law providing for the collection of revenue has not been created, that is to say, originated, by the Senate, in defiance of the seventh section of the first article of the Constitution, despite the permission given to the Senate to propose amendments. That which is *res adjudicata* [already judged] is no longer open to question. But one may safely hazard the opinion that none of the framers of the Constitution in discussing this clause of that instrument anticipated a day when a tariff bill framed by the House would be treated with contemptuous indifference by the Senate, and a tariff bill framed by the Senate would become the law of the land. But the fact is greater than the opinion. By the power of the Senate to amend, the preponderating control supposed to have been secured to the House by endowing it with the sole right to originate money bills, has been effaced. "They, in a word, hold the purse," Hamilton said of the House; but to-day the House holds the purse while the Senate dips into it.

The Senate and the House, therefore, stand on an equal footing, so far as the control of the public purse is concerned, the House having lost the ability to coerce the Senate by withholding supplies because the Senate by "amendment" can defy the House. But the Senate always has the advantage of the House in any contest, because of the fact that it is a small and well-disciplined body, and because of the feeling of superiority which belongs to the Senatorial estate. Objections have been frequently urged against the common use of the term "Upper House" as descriptive of the Senate, on the ground that, the Senate having coordinate and not greater privileges than the House, it is a mistake to give it an appellation that would signify superior authority. Technically, it is true that there is no distinction in the delegated powers, and yet the Constitution itself makes a distinction between the membership of the two Houses, requiring that the Senator shall be possessed of the wisdom that follows from greater age, and the more thorough comprehension of the spirit of the country proceeding from longer citizenship, if of alien birth. . . .

Senators Act in Their Own Interests

There is no way in which debate in the Senate can be abridged or terminated except by unanimous consent. . . . The majority governs only by the will of the minority. It is true that it does not always suit the purpose of the minority to exercise its power, but the power is latent and not surrendered. We have seen tariff bills "amended" by the Senate so that their framers did not recognize them; we have seen a single Senator compelling a majority to come to terms with him because he threatened to make a speech which it would take six weeks to deliver; we have seen a single Senator defeat a bill carrying an appropriation of some $70,000,000—a bill passed by the House and having a majority in its favor in the Senate—because it suited his purpose so to do.

It is because business in the Senate can only proceed by "unanimous consent" that the principle of "*Do ut des*" governs. A Senator who wants to secure an appropriation must not be too particular about some other Senator's little raid into the Treasury. Even great party measures can be brought to vote only by agreement. That is the reason why, during the course of a session, the *Congressional Record* has frequent mention of these agreements; that is why the announcement is repeatedly made that a vote will be considered as ordered on a certain bill on a definite day and hour, "if there be no objection," and no objection is ever made. A pact once made in the Senate is not broken. It is an agreement between gentlemen.

It has been shown that the Senate has equal power with the House over the control of appropriations; that it can create a tariff bill by the right of amendment; that it can prevent the enactment of any bill passed by the House; that it encourages members of the House to look for legislation in the Senate rather than in the House, where it rightfully belongs. One has never heard of Senators asking favors from Representatives.

To say that the House has been reduced to a negligible quantity in legislation would be an overstatement of the case; it is no exaggeration to say that it has become an insignificant factor. In further support of this assertion let it be said—and no greater practical proof of its correctness could be offered— that the correspondents who represent in Washington the leading newspapers of the country no longer think it necessary to consult members of the House regarding legislation; they confine their attention almost exclusively to the Senate. Time was, not many years ago, when important questions were pending, when the opinions of leaders in the House were as eagerly sought by these correspondents as were the opinions of leaders in the Senate, but to-day the mastery of the Senate is so clearly recognized that it would be a waste of time to seek for information elsewhere. When the important "Platt amendment" [concerning the withdrawal of U.S. troops from Cuba following the Spanish-American War of 1898] was under discussion last spring, scarcely a word was said, either in the newspapers or at the Capitol, about the attitude of the House. The same indifference as to the position of the House was displayed while the question was being argued whether the Philippines were to be governed by Congress or were for the time being to be left in the hands of the President.

Legislation, therefore, in Washington is represented by the Senate. Does the Senate dominate the President?

The Senate and the Presidency

Superficial observers are always fond of talking of the ease with which the President can control the Senate because he is the fountain head of patronage, unconsciously voicing the fear of Hamilton that "sometimes we are told that this fund of corruption is to be exhausted by the President in subduing the virtue of the Senate." Now, the fact is that the nature of the relations between the President and the Senate is very similar to the character of that *enfant terrible* [troublesome child] of our childhood whose virtues and faults have been celebrated in rhyme:

> "When she was good, she was very, very good, But when she was bad she was horrid."

Precisely so with the Senate. When President and Senate are on good terms, there is no more amiable legislative body in the world; but when the relations are strained the Senate can be extremely "horrid." Even in its most agreeable mood it constantly gives the President to understand that, while he may propose, the final disposition of measures of consequence rests with it. Allusion has been made to a single Senator defeating a great appropriation bill, and a few words of explanation will not be out of place as illustrating the control which individual Senators exercise over legislation. In the closing hours of the last session of Congress, Senator [Thomas Henry] Carter, of Montana, whose term expired with that Congress and who, therefore, was no longer bound by the obligations of "*Do ut des*," began a speech against the River and Harbor bill [which promised to require permits for discharging refuse into navigable waters]. That bill had already been passed by the House. Mr. Carter's opposition, it was said by some, was prompted by the President, who considered that the appropriation was extravagant; Mr. Carter, it was said by others, opposed the bill because no appropriation had been made to irrigate the arid lands of his own and adjacent States. It is quite immaterial what his motive was. In the closing hours of the night before the session terminated by constitutional limitation, Mr. Carter took the floor and began a semi-serious, semi-humorous speech against the bill. His purpose soon became obvious. Senators interested in the bill fumed and fidgeted; they implored and they even threatened; but Mr. Carter was adamantine. A few minutes before twelve o'clock on the fourth of March, when the session expired, Mr. Carter gracefully yielded the floor, and the bill was decently interred.

These same superficial observers, assuming that Mr. Carter had been instigated by the President, pointed to it as another evidence of the encroaching control of the President over legislation, forgetting that it was only another illustration of Senatorial power. If Mr. Carter could defeat a bill because it was not made up exactly in accordance with his views, why cannot Mr. Carter's successor do the same thing at this or any other session? In fact, he does not even have to exercise his power; it is quite sufficient for him to threaten to use it to gain his point. Mr. Carter has reminded his former colleagues that any Senator can shape any legislative act to accord with his ideas, provided he has the required determination. . . .

An Unwritten Code

What enables the oligarchs of the Senate to exercise their dominant power, to reduce the House to a legislative nonentity and to keep the President in subjection, is the peculiar code of the Senate, the unwritten code which is more powerful than the printed rules. The fear expressed by Hamilton, that a few of the members of the House by long experience and a mastery of public affairs would dominate their associates, finds its realization in the Senate. An *imperium in imperio* [empire within an empire] exists there. Despite the fact that all Senators are free and equal, that one man may be able to block business, and that "government by agreement" eliminates friction, all real authority is centered in a few hands; at

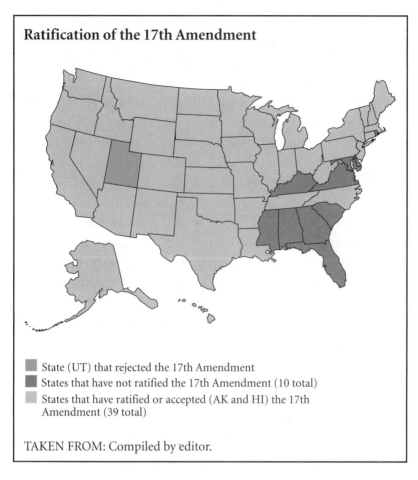

Ratification of the 17th Amendment

■ State (UT) that rejected the 17th Amendment
■ States that have not ratified the 17th Amendment (10 total)
■ States that have ratified or accepted (AK and HI) the 17th
Amendment (39 total)

TAKEN FROM: Compiled by editor.

the present time not more than half a dozen Senators have reached censorian dignity. The *Congressional Directory* of November 27th, 1900, a recent edition, gave the biographies of eighty-five Senators, there being five vacancies at that time. Of the total number, forty-eight were then serving their first term, nineteen their second, six their third, eight their fourth, and four their fifth; but even these figures are misleading, as some of the men credited with two terms have not seen six years of service; they were appointed to fill vacancies and then elected for a full term. But taking the figures as they stand, nearly eighty per cent. of the Senate has served less than twelve years and twenty per cent. more.

In the Senate authority comes with length of service. A new Senator is placed at the foot of unimportant committees, no matter how long his experience in public life or his standing in the House of Representatives or elsewhere, and he can only reach a chairmanship of a leading committee by the retirement of Senators who outrank him. The system is so automatic that it is almost military in its operation. No matter how brilliant the attainments of a captain, he must bow to the superior wisdom of a colonel or a general. A [Daniel] Webster entering the Senate to-day would perforce sit at the foot of the table and find it futile to try and oppose the chairman; and a Webster would find himself on a committee of minor importance, while men his intellectual inferiors and his juniors in years, but his seniors in service, would be members of great committees. By this method power always centers in the hands of a few men, the half dozen or so Senators who are at the head of the few really important committees. No legislation can be enacted, no policy can be put into execution, unless these men are first consulted and give their consent. They are, in effect, the Senate of the United States.

At the beginning of this article was used one of Bismarck's favorite maxims. Perhaps it may not be inappropriate to close with the remark made by the Iron Chancellor when discussing the terms of peace with France, an observation that the Senate might remember with profit: "*La patrie veut être servie, et non pas dominée*" [the nation wants to be useful, not dominate].

Senators Serve Powerful Financial Interests Instead of the American People

David Graham Phillips

One of the great motivations of those who favored the direct election of senators was their belief that such elections provided the best possible way to ensure that senators truly represented the people of their states rather than narrower interests. They found ammunition for their arguments in such articles as the following selection. In it, journalist David Graham Phillips examines the career of one senator, Arthur P. Gorman of Rhode Island (serving from 1881 to 1899 and 1903 to 1906). Phillips argues that Gorman represented important financial interests, such as the powerful Baltimore and Ohio Railroad of the day, rather than his constituents. He also claims that the Senate as a whole was a "machine" more concerned with protecting big business and with presenting an outward appearance of calm cooperation than with acting in the public interest.

A novelist as well as a journalist, David Graham Phillips (1867–1911) was one of a group of so-called muckrakers who sought to expose what they saw as the corruption and mismanagement of late nineteenth- and early twentieth-century America. The following selection is from a series of articles he published in Cosmopolitan Magazine *in 1906 titled* The Treason of the Senate. *The series is thought to have helped inspire the creation of the Seventeenth Amendment.*

We have now seen,

First: That there has been in the past quarter of a century an amazing and unnatural uppiling of wealth in the hands of

David Graham Phillips, "The Treason of the Senate," *Cosmopolitan Magazine*, vol. 41, no. 1, May 1906.

a few; that there has been an equally amazing and equally un-natural descent of the masses, despite skill and industry and the boundless resources of the country, toward the depen-dence of wages and salaries; that the massing of wealth and the diffusion of dependence are both swiftly increasing.

Second: That these abnormal conditions have come with, and out of, the development of a small group of controllers of railways and, through them, of finance and manufactures; that this little group controls and freely levies upon and trims the twenty thousand millions of our annual internal commerce, three-fourths of which is interstate and therefore subject to the supervision of Congress only.

Third: That this little group owes its power and its wealth, in part to legislation favoring it, but in the main to the failure of Congress to safeguard the people in the possession of the fruits of their labor by enacting the laws in regulation of in-terstate commerce which the public welfare has clearly de-manded and which the Constitution clearly authorizes.

Fourth: That the responsibility both for legislation in favor of "the interests" and for failure to legislate in restraint upon their depredations rests wholly and directly upon the United States Senate.

Fifth: That, as the Senate's legislation for "the interests" and its failure to legislate against them have not been frank and open, but tricky, stealthy and underhanded, the Senate cannot plead in its own defense either ignorance or honest motives; that its conduct has been and is deliberate, has been and is an intentional serving of "the interests" and an inten-tional betrayal of the people, has been and is treason.

Sixth: That the right arm of this treason has been and is Senator [Nelson W.] Aldrich [of Rhode Island, 1881–1911].

But the monster has a left arm, also. And that left arm, al-most as powerful and quite as useful as the right, is Arthur P. Gorman, of Maryland [1881–1899, 1903–1906].

Senate Serves Financial Interests

The common enemy, "the interests," dominate the political as well as the industrial machinery of the nation. In the political machinery of both parties they have at the important points faithful, well-paid agents, shrewd at fooling the people or at selecting those who can fool the people. Their control of state legislatures is such that they determine nearly three-fourths of the senators. Whoever may be, "for appearance's sake," in charge of the Republican machine, Aldrich is really in charge. Whoever may be nominally at the head of the Democratic machine, Gorman is really there. For only to men approved by them or their lieutenants will "the interests" supply the "oil" indispensable to a machine. Popular movements and heroes and spasms of reform rage and pass; but the machine abides, and after the storm it resumes; indeed, it works exceeding well even through the roughest cyclones. To our national political machine, with its label that reads "Republican" on the one side and "Democratic" on the other, Aldrich and Gorman are as the thumb and the forefinger to a skillful hand.

Gorman: From Page to "Patriot"

Gorman was born in Maryland sixty-seven years ago. After a few years at public school, he, at the age of thirteen, entered politics; his father, a contractor and lobbyist in a small way, got him a place as page in the United States Senate. This was in 1852, when the slave oligarchy [businessmen and politicians who wanted to maintain slavery], then in the heyday of its haughtiness, was using the same methods of sophistries about alleged "constitutional law" and alleged jealousy for the "grand old Constitution" that the industrial oligarchy is using in this heyday of its haughtiness. The slave oligarchy, to maintain and strengthen itself, was strenuous for the state as paramount over the nation; to-day, we have the doctrine resurrected by alleged Republicans from its grave under the battlefields of the

H. J. Res. 39.

Sixty-second Congress of the United States of America;

At the Second Session,

Begun and held at the City of Washington on Monday, the fourth day of December, one thousand nine hundred and eleven.

JOINT RESOLUTION

Proposing an amendment to the Constitution providing that Senators shall be elected by the people of the several States.

Resolved by the Senate and House of Representatives of the United States of America in Congress assembled (two-thirds of each House concurring therein), That in lieu of the first paragraph of section three of Article I of the Constitution of the United States, and in lieu of so much of paragraph two of the same section as relates to the filling of vacancies, the following be proposed as an amendment to the Constitution, which shall be valid to all intents and purposes as part of the Constitution when ratified by the legislatures of three-fourths of the States:

"The Senate of the United States shall be composed of two Senators from each State, elected by the people thereof, for six years; and each Senator shall have one vote. The electors in each State shall have the qualifications requisite for electors of the most numerous branch of the State legislatures.

"When vacancies happen in the representation of any State in the Senate, the executive authority of such State shall issue writs of election to fill such vacancies: *Provided,* That the legislature of any State may empower the executive thereof to make temporary appointments until the people fill the vacancies by election as the legislature may direct.

"This amendment shall not be so construed as to affect the election or term of any Senator chosen before it becomes valid as part of the Constitution."

Speaker of the House of Representatives.

Vice President of the United States and
President of the Senate.

The joint resolution pictured proposed the Seventeenth Amendment to the U.S. Constitution, which established the direct election of U.S. senators. National Archives & Records Administration.

Civil War, rehabilitated and restated to make the nation impotent before enemies far worse than the slave oligarchy. And under the renovated banner of "states' rights," "the blue" and "the gray," the "bloody shirt" Forakers and Spooners and the Confederate Baileys and Stones [earlier congressmen] march shoulder to shoulder in protecting "the interests" in their lootings.

Gorman, the brightest of bright boys, absorbed and assimilated all the mysteries of the Senate—all its crafty, treacherous ways of smothering, of emasculating, of perverting legislation; how to thwart the people and shift the responsibility; when to kill a just bill in committee and when to kill it in open Senate in the midst of a wild scrimmage among "honest patriots contending only for the right but conscientiously differing in views." For the Senate, not elected by the people, not responsible to them, and containing a controlling nucleus of men who have their seats as securely and for as long a period as the members of any hereditary legislative body in the world—the Senate has almost from the beginning been the bulwark of whatever form of privilege happened to be struggling to maintain itself against the people.

Tricks and Questionable Loyalties

Gorman continued his invaluable education in the Senate throughout the stormy, corrupt days of the Civil War. In 1866 he received from a Republican President the internal-revenue collectorship for the Fifth Maryland District. It has been charged that he was in those days a Republican, and that this appointment is proof of it. But the charge is foolish. He was no more a Republican then than he is a Democrat now. Such men have no politics of principle; and no one will think they have if he will take the trouble to glance from the badge to the man and his deeds. In the spring of 1869, Gorman ceased to be a Republican officeholder; in the fall he was elected to the lower house of the Maryland legislature by the Democratic party. There, at the age of thirty, he entered upon his real career.

Aldrich's simple home problem has been to rule Rhode Island by means of an aristocratic old constitution which puts all the power in the hands of the ignorant and cheaply purchaseable voters of a few sparsely populated rural townships. Gorman's has been less easy, yet far from difficult. Maryland, being a border state, has a great many white Republicans; and there is a negro vote large enough to hold the balance of power. It has been Gorman's cue to keep "negro domination" ever before the eyes of the Maryland voter, to make the whites feel that, rotten though his machine is, it is yet the only alternative to "rule by and for the black." When the Republican machine, usually his docile dependent, would in some brief spasm of reform cease to play his game, he has sometimes lost; not always, because the uncertain conditions in Baltimore compelled the machine to maintain at all times an army of thugs, repeaters, ballot-box stuffers and the like, and several times the lost day has been saved to him by a carnival of ballot-box debauchery and bloody rioting.

Not Challenging His Critics

In a speech in Baltimore, on October 15, 1895, [future president] Theodore Roosevelt said,

> "I caught Mr. Gorman in an ugly falsehood, one that might be termed better in the plain Anglo-Saxon word of three letters [i.e., 'lie']."

Mr. Bonaparte, the present secretary of the navy said on March 31, 1904:

> "A good many years ago Mr. Gorman was described on good Democratic authority as a 'generalissimo of the lobby.' Senator Gorman calls me a professional reformer. Whether

it is more commendable to be a professional reformer or a professional lobbyist I must leave each to judge for himself. But I must own that Senator Gorman's 'profession' has had one advantage over mine—it has been vastly more profitable. Although the senator seems to think honesty is of minor importance in determining a man's qualifications for high public office, it is certainly true that a conspicuous absence of this qualification has not proved fatal to at least one man holding a high office and aspiring to a higher." (Gorman was then a seeker of the nomination for President.)

On October 22, 1888, Henry E Wooten, a distinguished Marylander living at Ellicott City, issued an open letter to Gorman in which he challenged him to sue for libel on the following statements:

"That you, with your own hands, assisted by others, distributed three thousand dollars among the ruffians that thronged the city in 1875."

"That you were an active participant in the fraud of 1879. You had [political crony Eugene] Higgins at your headquarters in Baltimore, and he was in this county at least upon two occasions closeted with you and other conspirators against the rights and liberties of the people, perfecting the details of the conspiracy, conferring as to what names should be dropped and what names misspelled, and by which route the negro repeaters should be sent out."

"That you are steeped in corruption and saturated with official perjury."

Gorman did not sue Mr. Wooten for calling him a briber and perjurer. Nor did he sue Mr. Roosevelt for calling him a liar, nor Mr. Bonaparte for calling him a notoriously dishonest professional lobbyist. Nor did he sue Bernard Carter, the eminent lawyer and Democrat, who denounced him as "generalissimo of the lobby" when he was handing over the streets of

Baltimore to the Baltimore and Ohio Railroad, which was the section of "the interests" he chiefly represented in those days. . . .

The Black Art of Politics

Gorman entered the Senate as a senator twenty-five years ago this spring [1906]. He already knew the mysteries of the Senate. He had been studying and practicing the black art of politics for nearly thirty years. Inevitably he was soon a leader, the trusted counselor of those of his party who wished to be led skillfully in the subtle ways of doing the will of "the interests" without inflaming the people against them. He, of course, entered the Senate primarily as an agent of the eminently respectable among his pals and sponsors, the interstate looters through the railway corporations of his state. Every traitor senator, whatever else he represents in the way of an enemy to the people, always represents some thief or group of thieves through railways. For the railway, reaching everywhere, as intimate a part of our life now as the air we breathe, is the easy and perfect instrument of the wholesale looter of investors and of the public, and is also the natural nucleus and subsidizer of a political machine. And, as the railways have merged—even Aldrich now publicly concedes that competition has been almost abolished—the senators have "merged" also. And peace reigns in the Senate Chamber under a "community of interest" in treason corresponding to the "community of interest" in spoliation.

But it is with the "merging" of the Republican and Democratic political machines that we are now concerned. And let no one be distracted by the roaring eloquence and the sham battles of the Senate or by the "eminent respectability" of the senators into losing sight of the central fact that the machines, drawing their revenues from the one power, ruled by the twin agents of that power, are the property of that power—never more so than when the politicians, wearing and disgracing official robes, beat the air and "jam the wind" to make the people confuse party and party principle with party machine. To appreciate the Senate look, not at its professions, not at the surface pretenses of the measures it permits to become laws, but at the effect of those laws—how plutocracy and plunder thrive under them. And to understand why the laws always somehow fail to serve the people, always somehow relicense the people's enemies, look at Aldrich and Gorman and their band—how they got, how they keep their seats; whom they associate with; their private fortunes; how their fortunes are invested. "Where a man's treasure is, there will his heart be also."

Rarely does the Senate hold a session without there cropping out some indication of the existence of this secret "merger" of the two party machines under which they work together in harmony wherever "the interests" are interested—befogging the responsibility for acts hostile to the public interest, lining up senators from both parties for a debate or a vote, and releasing to perfunctory, though always perfervid opposition, senators who have "insuperable conscientious objections" in the particular matter or dare not offend the people of their state in that particular crisis. For, while many of the "merged" senators can all but leave out of account the feelings of "my people," there are more who have to be "conscientious" and careful and crafty, except during the first two or three years after they have been elected, and when they have three or four years before they come up for election again. Occasionally the evidences of the existence and smooth working of the "merger" are so plain that only the very stupid or the stone-blind partisan would fail to see.

Advocates of the Seventeenth Amendment Hoped That It Would Minimize Corruption

Lewis L. Gould

In the following selection, historian Lewis L. Gould describes the Seventeenth Amendment as being part of a wave of reforms that began after the congressional elections of 1910, which resulted in Democratic majorities in both houses. These reforms continued, following the election of Democratic president Woodrow Wilson in 1912.

By 1910, the momentum toward the Seventeenth Amendment was powerful, strengthened both by moves in individual states toward direct election of senators and by the growing sense that the Senate, as it was then organized, was both elitist and corrupt. But, when late that year and throughout 1911 Congress debated the proposed amendment, new issues arose. One of the important and contentious issues, as Gould notes, was the African American vote. Some Congressmen, who feared the results of African American votes in senatorial elections, forced through a provision in the amendment that would allow states, rather than the U.S. Congress, to establish the actual rules for senatorial elections. Still, despite the compromises, those who favored the Seventeenth Amendment believed it would do a great deal to truly democratize the Senate. Lewis L. Gould is an emeritus professor of history at the University of Texas–Austin and a fellow at the university's Center for American History as well as the author of many books and articles.

Lewis L. Gould, *The Most Exclusive Club: A History of the Modern United States Senate*. Cambridge, MA: Basic Books, 2005. Copyright © 2005 by Lewis L. Gould. All rights reserved. Reprinted by permission of Basic Books, a member of Perseus Books, L.L.C.

For the Senate, a creative burst of energy occurred in the six years following the Democratic election victories in 1910. In that span, the upper house adopted a constitutional amendment for the direct election of senators, approved the Federal Reserve Act, passed the income tax, and enacted the social justice legislation that President Woodrow Wilson proposed.

The service of the new Democratic senators who won seats in 1910 began in April 1911, when President [William Howard] Taft summoned lawmakers into a special session. The session's main purpose was to deal with the president's proposal for a reciprocal tariff agreement with Canada. When they assembled for that task, the senators soon faced a showdown on the constitutional amendment to provide for direct election of senators.

Since 1905, states had sought various ways to require legislatures to accept the winner of a party primary as their choice for the Senate. As these procedures evolved, they generated pressure on the Senate to adopt an amendment for the direct election of senators. Adding to the urgency that members felt was mounting evidence of corruption in the way some states chose senators. For example, when John Coit Spooner left the Senate in 1907, the governor of Wisconsin appointed Isaac Stephenson to succeed him. Two years later, the elderly, wealthy Stephenson won the Republican primary for a full term. His opponents charged that he had spread money around during the primary contest to make sure of his victory. Challenges to the legality of his election went before the Senate.

Responding to Scandal

Yet what happened in Wisconsin stirred less popular clamor than did the controversy over the election of William Lorimer of Illinois in 1909. Once the "Blond Boss" of Chicago politics, Lorimer had faded as a player in the city's public life, but then was unexpectedly chosen for the Senate after the legislature had deadlocked over other hopefuls. Lorimer became a conservative ally of [powerful Rhode Island senator] Nelson Aldrich in Washington.

Then the scandal broke. In late April 1910, a Democratic member of the Illinois Assembly told a Chicago newspaper that he had been bribed to vote for Lorimer. Banner headlines made the charge a national controversy. A Senate subcommittee of the Senate Privileges and Elections Committee looked into the matter and exonerated Lorimer of wrongdoing. In December 1910, the full Senate confirmed that result by a vote of 46 to 40, but that ballot was not the end of the Lorimer battle. His enemies continued to gather evidence of scandal in his election, and the battle over his right to hold the seat raged in the national press.

Meanwhile, proponents of direct elections pressed for action on the amendment. Joseph L. Bristow of Kansas had been pushing the amendment for two years without making much progress. In the wake of the Lorimer affair, the Judiciary Committee agreed to name a subcommittee to consider the resolution to adopt the amendment at the end of December 1910. Their deliberations led to language about direct election in a proposed amendment but with important new wording. Southern senators, fearful that the federal government might enforce the voting rights of African Americans, wanted a concession. They insisted on adding a provision that would strip the Congress of the power to provide rules for senatorial elections, as specified in the Constitution, and would cede it to the states.

The Seventeenth Amendment and Race

The always lurking race issue now flared up. Republicans sought to amend the Bristow resolution by deleting the wording that the South wanted about Senate elections. Concern for

African-American rights was one element in their thinking. In addition, conservatives who disliked direct elections knew that the removal of the provision about state control of Senate elections would make southerners less likely to vote for the underlying principle. On the floor, Republicans complained that ceding jurisdiction over Senate contests to the states "would give substantial though limited sanction to the disfranchisement of Negroes in the Southern states." In February 1911, the Republicans' wording for the amendment was adopted. The resolution for a constitutional amendment then failed to obtain a two-thirds majority.

With Taft's special session, the direct-election amendment reappeared, as its proponents seized the chance to see it passed in a more sympathetic Senate. Bristow proposed to his colleagues that they drop the language about states controlling Senate elections and just support the principle of having the voters elect senators. There was a tie on this vote, and Vice President James S. Sherman cast the deciding ballot in favor of Bristow's position. Both houses had now approved the amendment, but southerners in the House insisted on removal of the election control provision from the Constitution. Eleven months passed before the House yielded and agreed to the Senate version, on May 11, 1912. The amendment then went to the states for ratification.

The larger purpose of the amendment, in the minds of Bristow and Idaho's William E. Borah, was that direct elections could be "the most effective means of taking from organized wealth the control of the Senate, and indeed our national politics." The quality of the upper house would also be improved once the people themselves would choose their senators. The fervor to have senators elected in this way grew out of the dislike for political parties that animated middle-class Americans during these years. Having legislatures designate senators was inherently undemocratic; now the people would rule. Once the amendment was ratified, as everyone knew it would be, this political optimism would be put to the test.

The Seventeenth Amendment Inspired Passionate Debate in the Senate

The New York Times

The following selection is an article from the New York Times *on February 18, 1911. It reports on the debates in the Senate then under way on what form the Seventeenth Amendment might take. The article makes clear that the debate was contentious, with at least one senator willing to use a filibuster to keep it from reaching a vote. Among the important issues the article touches on is the proposal that the amendment include a provision, introduced by Senator George Sutherland of Utah, allowing the U.S. Congress to set the rules for senatorial elections in the individual states. Senators from southern states, and even from border states such as Maryland, feared that such a provision would allow the federal government to act to protect the voting rights of African Americans. Many of these senators, therefore, pledged to oppose the amendment.*

Washington, Feb. 17.—The Senate devoted the whole of today's session to debate on the popular election of Senators without apparently getting any nearer a vote. Mr. Borah of Idaho, who is in charge of the resolution, made a dozen proposals for an agreement to vote, but his colleague, Mr. Heyburn, resolutely objected. Mr. Heyburn is determined to prevent action this session, and for the present there are enough Senators anxious to discuss the measure to make a solitary filibuster effective.

Mr. Heyburn has a double purpose. He is bitterly opposed to direct elections, though instructed to support the measure

Special to *The New York Times*, "Fails to Force Vote on Direct Elections," *The New York Times*, February 18, 1911.

by his Legislature. He is equally opposed to Canadian reciprocity [a tariff agreement]. Filibustering against one of these measures is filibustering against the other, and he has practically given notice of his intention to talk until March 4.

In his effort to force a vote Mr. Borah tried hard to keep the Senate in continuous session, so that his opponents should either have to talk forever or yield to a roll call. Mr. Gallinger late in the afternoon made a motion to adjourn, but it was defeated 44 to 36. A few minutes later, however, Senator Nelson, who had waited all day to speak, made a plea for a night's rest before beginning, and Senatorial courtesy caused the adoption of a motion for an executive session, which was soon adjourned.

It is now likely that the measure will remain before the Senate for some time to come. To-morrow, after 2:30 o'clock, the session will be devoted to eulogies of dead members, and the same order will obtain on Monday. Mr. Beveridge has given notice that on Tuesday he will try to force a vote on the Lorimer question [a corruption case against Senator Lorimer of Illinois] and that may run over until next day.

The Negro Vote in Southern States

Debate on popular elections began as soon as the Senate had concluded its routine business to-day. Senator Rayner began it with opposition to the Sutherland amendment, which would give control over Senatorial elections to Congress instead of the State Legislatures. This amendment is opposed by Southern Senators because it might lead to Federal action to insure votes to negroes. Mr. Rayner contended that even without the Sutherland provision the Federal Government would have the right to protect voters against fraud or intimidation. He appealed to supporters of the original proposition not to burden it with any amendment which would imperil the success of the resolution itself.

"Why would it imperil the resolution?" asked Mr. Nelson.

"Because," said Mr. Rayner "it would affect a large number of members on the Democratic side of the chamber who would vote against the proposition with the Sutherland amendment incorporated in it."

"Why should they vote against it?" asked Mr. Nelson.

"I am not a mind reader and cannot undertake to say," Mr. Rayner replied. "If the Senator will visit this side he will find out. But I am sure that the amendment will weaken the resolution. We need a two-thirds vote to adopt the resolution and cannot afford to take chances."

Mr. Rayner warned the Senate against any interference with the franchise [the right to vote] regulations of the Southern States, which insured the supremacy of the white race in the South. For the protection of its own membership the Senate could not afford a change, he urged.

"It is for your own welfare and for the welfare of the Union," he said, "that the South should maintain her institutions from the invader's touch, and that you should keep your hands off the pillars of the temple."

Senator Carter said that if the color line had been brought into the debate, it had been done by the Senators who sought to change the Constitution. He would not concede that without a provision like the Sutherland amendment the Constitution would protect men in the exercise of the franchise. While there might not now be any disposition to interfere in the perplexing difficulties which confronted the people of the South, still there was no desire forever to deprive the negro of the protection of the general Government.

Mr. Rayner, speaking with much vehemence, declared that Mr. Carter was "bitterly opposed to the election of Senators by the people." Mr. Carter objected to the statement, and Mr. Rayner substituted "cheerfully" for "bitterly." Mr. Carter still objected, and Mr. Rayner asked what his attitude was. He then admitted that it was his intention to vote for direct elections because his Legislature had instructed him to do so, but otherwise he would be against the plan.

Mr. Heyburn spoke at length in opposition to the entire effort to amend the Constitution. Referring to a resolution of his own State Legislature instructing him to vote for the proposition, he declared that he could not comply with the instructions.

"A man who is afraid of his Legislature or whose vote is affected by what his Legislature may do is not fit to be here," he said.

The Seventeenth Amendment Was the Work of a Small Group of Congressional "Progressives"

A. Bower Sageser

During the first decades of the twentieth century, the United States went through a period known as the Progressive Era. Progressives of the era favored a wide variety of political reforms. They were populists who believed that governments should be more responsive to ordinary people. They also wanted to reduce the power of big business by breaking up the "trusts" that provided for monopoly control of some industries as well as by strengthening labor unions. They also, variously, stood for women's rights, the establishment of public health programs, and even environmentalism.

In the following selection, historian A. Bower Sageser argues that the Seventeenth Amendment was part of this wave of progressivism. Those who were most aggressive in moving the amendment through Congress, he says, were progressive senators such as Joseph L. Bristow of Kansas (served 1909–1915) and his colleague William E. Borah of Idaho (served 1907–1940). A. Bower Sageser was professor of history at Kansas State University.

The decision that the junior senator from Kansas would carry the workload for the direct election of senators undoubtedly led to one of [Joseph L.] Bristow's major contributions to American government. The idea of the selection of senators by direct vote was nearly a century old: it was first introduced into Congress in 1826. By 1909 approximately forty resolutions involving the idea had been introduced into Congress. Members of the House were more sympathetic toward adoption than were senators; in the Senate it was difficult to secure a favorable report from the Committee on Privileges and Elections, the committee to which the proposal was most frequently referred. During his first month in the Senate, Bristow had proposed the modification of Section 3 of the Constitution to allow for the direct election of senators by the people. He tied his proposal to [Iowa] Senator [Albert D.] Cummins' income tax proposal; both failed at that time. In the next congressional session Bristow turned to a direct amendment to the Constitution, but . . . Bristow had to work persistently for three years before his amendment became the fundamental law of the land.

Moving Through the Senate

Friends encouraged Bristow to assign his proposal to the Judiciary Committee, where it might receive more favorable treatment. Once assigned, it was not reported out of the committee for nearly sixteen months, in spite of Bristow's use of every parliamentary device at his disposal. The proposed amendment called for national supervision of the election of senators on the same basis as in elections of members to the House of Representatives, and a bitter fight was led by southern Democrats over the right of the states to control the election of senators. After considerable maneuvering the progressives placed [Idaho] Senator [William E.] Borah on a subcommittee of the Judiciary Committee. Through hard work Borah eventually got the Bristow resolution to the floor of the Senate, in February, 1911, but the resolution was defeated.

Ten United States senators who had voted against the Bristow proposal in 1909 were retired in the election of 1910, and six newly elected senators favored the amendment. Bristow debated the issue in the spring of 1911. He was greatly encouraged in his fight when the Kansas legislature, in February, 1911, adopted a resolution urging its representatives and senators in Washington to support the proposal. Little that was new could be added to the debate, which had been current since Populist days [i.e., the last quarter of the nineteenth century]. Bristow pointed out that thirty-three state legislatures had declared in favor, in substance if not in form, and four states had primary laws nominating senators by general election. He emphasized his great trust in the people's ability to select senators, in contrast with the views held in the early days of the Republic, maintaining that direct election would free the state legislatures from pressure and corruption and the country from greed and vested interests.

Senator Borah secured a favorable report from the Judiciary Committee again on May 8, 1911, and on June 12, 1911, the Senate adopted the amendment by a vote of 64 to 24. Bristow wrote to [a Kansas associate] on May 14 that it was "exceedingly gratifying" to be the author of the first change in the fundamental law on representation since the early period of the Republic. The New York *Tribune* praised Bristow's work, declaring that his opposition to state control of elections saved the entire proposition from defeat. [Progressive congressmen] William Jennings Bryan and Champ Clark brought pressure on members of the House of Representatives, and the House accepted the proposal by a vote of 237 to 12 on May 13, 1912.

Ensuring Ratification by the States

Bristow had done a signal job in keeping the issue before the Senate, but his task was not completed. State legislative approval had to follow. In February, 1913, Bristow shouldered the task of writing to all the secretaries of state and lieutenant governors to see if the proposed amendment was being considered. He was pleased when the name of his home state came in among the first twelve favorable responses. As each state fell into line, he sent new letters to those that had not acted. By February 21 twenty-three states had acted favorably; the number rose to thirty-one by March 13, 1913. Bristow now called upon William Jennings Bryan, who had become United States Secretary of State, to exert pressure on his friends, especially in Delaware, New Jersey, Connecticut, and Rhode Island. Connecticut was the thirty-third state to approve, and by April 9 thirty-six states had reported in favor. On that day Bristow wrote to Theodore Roosevelt that the seventeenth amendment was "now a part of the Constitution." He continued, "I think it is the most fundamental change in the Constitution that has been made and it is the first direct progressive achievement."

Although, throughout the land newspapers supporting the issue credited the victory to the tireless and faithful work of Senators Bristow and Borah, Bristow was not invited to the final ceremonies held by Bryan and President Wilson to amend the Constitution. Bryan brought in former Congressman [Henry St. George] Tucker of Virginia, a Democrat who had introduced a similar resolution twenty years before, and credited him with the accomplishment. The claim that this was a victory for the Democrats was a weak one, considering that only one Democrat in the Senate had voted for the amendment in the spring of 1911. Bristow was bitter over his failure to get recognition, but he did not speak out because he did not want to start a quarrel with the new administration. Although the newly elected Democrats laid false claim to responsibility for the seventeenth amendment, the midwestern Republican leadership had won credit for the adoption of the sixteenth amendment, the income tax amendment, on February 25, 1913.

CONSTITUTIONAL
AMENDMENTS
BEYOND THE BILL OF RIGHTS

CHAPTER 2

Calls to Repeal or Change the Seventeenth Amendment

The Seventeenth Amendment Has Made the Senate Less Effective

George H. Haynes

The Senate is conventionally considered the "upper" house of the United States Congress where each state, regardless of its population, sends two officials who serve longer terms (six years) than even presidents do. By contrast, the House of Representatives, the "lower" house, is considered to more directly reflect the American people because the number of any state's representatives depends on that state's population. In addition, members of the House serve only two-year terms before seeking reelection.

In the following selection historian George H. Haynes argues that the Seventeenth Amendment weakened both the status and effectiveness of the upper house of the U.S. Congress. By requiring senators to stand in popular elections, he maintains, senators are distracted from the "cool and courageous exercise of [their] distinctive powers." Writing in 1938, twenty-five years after the ratification of the Seventeenth Amendment, Haynes claimed to see a decline in the Senate's confidence that was not balanced by any noticeable gain in Congress's lawmaking ability. Haynes, author of The Senate of the United States: Its History and Practice, *was for decades considered the primary academic historian of the upper house of Congress.*

As early as 1896, in a formal report a Senate committee deplored the fact that 'the tendency of public opinion is to disparage and depreciate its [the Senate's] usefulness, its integrity, its power.' It chanced that in 1910 upon the same day the press announced that after thirty years of service in the Senate both [Eugene] Hale and [Nelson] Aldrich had decided not to stand for re-election. By that time the ratification of a popular-election amendment was clearly foreseen. There was much editorial comment upon the 'vanishing type' represented by these two powerful Senators. They were men of great ability— one principally an obstructionist, the other a construction-ist—yet for the most part using their ability with rather con-temptuous disdain of common folk's concerns, but with keen attention to the wants of 'big business.'

So far as its effects upon the state legislatures are con-cerned, the Seventeenth Amendment did bring much-needed reforms: it put an end to the blurring of issues in the election of members of the legislatures, and to the prolonged dead-locks which often distracted and delayed, if they did not actu-ally prevent, the doing of the essential tasks of lawmaking and providing the means for carrying on the state governments. But in some other respects, if one may judge by the com-ments of many Senators, the success of this 'epoch-making reform' has not been so obvious.

Did the Seventeenth Amendment Work?

In debating a resolution to amend the Constitution so as to give to the people of the several states the power by their di-rect vote to ratify or to reject future amendments, the Sena-tors, some ten years after the adoption of the popular-election amendment, found themselves led into a discussion of its suc-cess or failure. A delicate question, that, for the Senate Cham-ber! Said [Ohio senator Simeon] Fess: 'Whether or not we have elevated the standard of this body by the change in the manner of the election of Senators, is still an open question. . . . I have come to have serious doubts as to whether or not the change has been beneficial.' [Senator David] Reed (Pennsylvania) gave as one reason 'why the Seventeenth

Amendment is not a success' the fact that 'so small a proportion of the citizenry takes advantage of the opportunities that it gives. . . . I think on the whole the Amendment has not worked anything like as well as we had hoped.' [Senator Joseph] Robinson (Arkansas), later Democratic majority leader in the Senate, declared: 'The Seventeenth Amendment probably accomplished no permanent improvement in the national system of lawmaking.'

There can be no question that in the years since the ratification of the Seventeenth Amendment the prestige of the Senate has suffered serious decline. To say this is by no means equivalent to saying that the Senate has deteriorated. But the mere fact of the lessened esteem and confidence in which the Senate has come to be held is greatly to be deplored. There has been no period in our history when there was more need for the cool and courageous exercise of the Senate's distinctive powers of revision and amendment, of confirmation and ratification, and of investigation, than in the years since the people took into their own hands the direct election of Senators.

The Senate is restive under criticism, especially when it comes from those that are of its own household, whether members or officers. Senators who in the above debate expressed their doubts as to whether the standard of the Senate had been raised by popular election at once laid themselves open to reproach and derision by their colleagues.

Lower Prestige

Most eloquent and aggressive in defense of the Senate against adverse criticism has been Senator David I. Walsh [Massachusetts]. In his opinion 'the United States Senate is the last citadel of minority rights, and the protector of weaker states.' Raising the question, 'Has the Senate deteriorated?' he replied:

> Yes, if the measure by which you judge the value and usefulness of a legislative body is the worldly possessions of its

Senator David I. Walsh was known for his aggressive and eloquent defense against critics of the Seventeenth Amendment and the Senate. Thomas D. McAvoy/Time & Life Pictures/ Getty Images.

members—or if you estimate a legislative body by its culture and social refinements—or by the personal record of its members as attorneys for or representatives of large business interests before entering public life.

In his opinion the only test which it is fair to apply in determining whether the Senate is or is not deteriorating is 'the moral seriousness of its members—that moral seriousness which includes industry, integrity, and a serious consciousness of the grave responsibilities of public service.' The real reason 'for the propaganda against the Senate . . . for the efforts to spread the delusion that its personnel has deteriorated since the Senators have been directly elected by the people,' he finds is 'the presence in that body of a new, substantial, aggressive, independent, and progressive type and spirit.'

> The Senate has defects. Let us correct them with sympathetic hands. The Senate has imperfections. Let us purge it of them, and the Senate will be a stronger bulwark than ever of our liberties. Let us stop abusing it, because it is not controlled as well by political bosses and financial groups as formerly. In any event, all who sit here have been sent here by the American people. An indictment of the Senate is an indictment of the whole people.

After eight years of close observation of the Senate, at first from the chair of its presiding officer and later from the White House, ex-President [Calvin] Coolidge [1923–29] wrote: 'While I do not share altogether the prevailing lack of esteem in which the Senate is held, I fully realize the need of sending to that Chamber men of ability, character, and training.' That the Senate is held in a 'prevailing lack of esteem' is a fact as unfortunate as it is indisputable. It is a fact to be frankly faced, and not to be put aside by oratorical denial of the fact, nor by denunciation of those who state it. Instead of alleging or denying that the Senate has 'deteriorated,' it is better worth while to seek some of the causes of that 'lack of esteem,' and some of the conditions which are making it difficult to send to the Senate men of that 'moral seriousness' and of 'the ability, character, and training' recognized by Senator Walsh and ex-President Coolidge alike as highly essential for eminent service in the Senate.

In the first place, as [President] Woodrow Wilson wrote many years ago:

> The Senate is just what the mode of its election and the conditions of public life in this country make it. . . .

> The Senate is in fact, of course, nothing more than a part, though a considerable part, of the public service, and if the general conditions of that service be such as to starve states-men and foster demagogues, the Senate itself will be full of the latter kind, simply because there are no others available. There cannot be a separate breed of public men reared specially for the Senate. It contains the most perfect product of our politics, whatever that product may be.

In the second place, the Senator's tasks in recent years have become much more difficult and complicated. The problems with which the Senate now deals are mainly economic; in a world of rapid change their solution is increasingly becoming involved in international readjustments.

Distracted by Elections

Furthermore, the Senator's work must now be done amid incessant distractions necessary in maintaining satisfactory contacts with his constituents, that his days may be long in the seat which they gave him. No intelligent man who had actual knowledge of the election of Senators by state legislatures would wish to see a return to a method which proved itself subject to the grave abuses which led to its abandonment. Popular election has eliminated some of the worst features of the earlier method, but it has developed serious defects of its own which need frank recognition and correction. The Senate has shown no great zeal for the correcting of these defects 'with sympathetic hands,' though Senator Walsh is to be credited with initiating important legislation directed to that end. Most of these defects are associated with the direct primary which has revealed ineffective and dangerous possibilities hardly suspected when it was being heralded as the panacea [cure-all] for democracy's ills.

In theory the direct primary and popular election of Senators are supposed to exemplify pure democracy: We, the alert, intelligent, and incorruptible voters, sign nomination papers for those whom we—from our own personal knowledge or from careful study of reliable information—believe to be best qualified for senatorial service. In the primary there emerge the few candidates of most convincing qualifications. In the election, 'majority (?) rules,' and 'the voice of the People is the voice of God.' Unfortunately, in actual practice the procedure and the result are often 'quite other.'

A Senator's most valuable and statesmanlike work is usually entirely undramatic. [Kentucky senator] Henry Clay declared that he 'did infinitely more in his room than he did in the Senate Chamber,' for in the quiet of his own room 'he was at work night and day, either reading, digesting, or preparing matters in connection with his public duties.' But the public cannot properly appraise the value of this preparatory work in the Senator's own study, nor his diligence and effectiveness in the committee room where most of the analytical and discriminating work of lawmaking is done. For essential but routine service such as this, the would-be candidate is not likely to have given evidence of special qualifications. That a man has a nimble tongue and can make a stirring stump speech, that he has made a sensational 'success' as a prosecuting attorney, that he has attained nation-wide recognition or notoriety as a state governor—any or all of these 'records' may afford no proof of his fitness for eminent service in the Senate. Of the men, chosen by direct primary and elected by popular vote, who in recent years have been most responsible for 'the prevailing lack of esteem in which the Senate is held,' several had loomed large in the headlines as prosecuting attorneys or governors.

The Seventeenth Amendment Has Inspired a Wave of Federalist Decisions in the U.S. Supreme Court

John Dean

In the following selection, John Dean examines one of the unforeseen effects of the Seventeenth Amendment. Dean claims that during the tenure of U.S. Chief Justice William Rehnquist, who was appointed to the post in 1994 and served there until his death in 2005, it was indeed the Supreme Court, rather than the Senate, that devoted most attention to federalism, the relationship between individual states and the national government. Citing the opinions of other scholars as well as asserting his own, Dean argues that the Seventeenth Amendment, along with other measures, amounted to an expansion in the power of the national government and a concurrent lessening of emphasis on states' rights. Such an expansion was especially vivid with the assertions of government authority following the September 2001 terrorist attacks in New York City and Washington, D.C. To Dean's mind the Rehnquist Court, despite its conservative bent, stepped in to fill the void and defend states' rights. John Dean served as special counsel to President Richard M. Nixon from 1970 to 1973. He is the author of many books on American law, history, and current events.

Federalism—the allocation and balancing of power between state and federal government—has emerged as a central concern of the Supreme Court under Chief Justice William Rehnquist. Slowly, but steadily, the Rehnquist Court has been cutting back federal powers, and protecting state's rights.

John Dean, "The 17th Amendment: Should It Be Repealed," The Lawful Path, September 13, 2002. Reprinted by permission of FindLaw.com, a Thomson Reuters company.

Many have wondered what the Court is doing. Why are the Court's five conservatives—the Chief Justice himself, along with Associate Justices Sandra Day O'Connor, Antonin Scalia, Anthony Kennedy, and Clarence Thomas—creating this new jurisprudence of federalism?

The answer is simple: they are seeking to fill a void in our constitutional structure, a problem created early in the Twentieth Century. The problem began when, in the name of "democracy," we tinkered with the fundamental structure of the Constitution by adopting the Seventeenth Amendment.

The Amendment calls for direct election of U.S. Senators. It's a change that has in fact proved anything but democratic. And it is a change whose aftermath may haunt the Twenty-first Century.

Concerns About Federalism

Divisions of power are rooted in our Constitution. Experience had taught the Framers the dangers of concentrations of ruling authority, resulting in their ingenious template of checks and balances, with divisions and distributions of power.

Ultimate power in a democracy resides with the people. We are not a pure democracy, however, but rather a confederated republic (one that features, as well, county and local political subdivisions).

Thus, while there is national sovereignty, there is also state sovereignty. Power has been so divided and spread for one reason: to provide for and protect the highest sovereignty—that of each individual citizen.

Only fools reject the wisdom of this founding principle of diffusing power. Yet from the outset there has been debate regarding the appropriate allocation and balancing of these powers. The debate has focussed on not only whether a particular matter should be dealt with at the state versus the national level, but also on how these allocations are adjusted from time to time.

John Dean, author and former White House counsel to President Richard Nixon, believes the Seventeenth Amendment lessened the emphasis on states' rights. © David Scull/epa/ Corbis.

Of late, for example, along with laments for those who tragically lost their lives during the September 11th terrorist attack, there has been widespread concern with new realignments of federal/state powers that have followed in the name of homeland security.

Most significantly, Washington is assuming powers that have only previously existed during a Congressionally declared war.

The Framers' Bicameralism

In designing our Constitutional system, the Framers sought to remedy the limits of the Articles Of Confederation, which created a loose association of states with little central power. The new system, they decided, ought to feature a better allocation of powers—and the federal government should have the powers "necessary and proper" to perform its envisaged functions. The will of the People should be the foundation, and the foundational institution should be the law-making legislative branch.

Unsurprisingly, the Revolutionaries were not very impressed with most aspects of the British model of government. They rejected parliamentary government, with its king or queen and three estates of the realm (lords spiritual, lords temporal, and the commons).

But one feature of the British system, the Framers did borrow. That was bicameralism—a word coined by Brit Jeremy Bentham to describe the division of the legislature into two chambers (or, in Latin, *camera*).

The British Parliament had its House of Lords as the upper chamber and the House of Commons as the lower chamber. Citizens selected members of the House of Commons. The members of the House of Lords, in contrast, were those who had been titled by a king or queen (lords temporal) and the archbishops and bishops of the Church of England (lords spiritual).

Loosely basing our bicameral legislature on this model (minus the lords, both temporal and spiritual), the Framers created the House of Representatives as the lower chamber, whose members would be selected directly by the people. And with almost unanimous agreement, they determined that members of the upper chamber, the Senate, would be selected not directly, but by the legislatures of the states. Each state would have two Senators, while Representatives would be apportioned based on population.

[Founder father] James Madison was not only involved in structuring the system, but was also a keeper of its contemporaneous record. He explained in Federalist [Paper] No. 10 the reason for bicameralism: "Before taking effect, legislation would have to be ratified by two independent power sources: the people's representatives in the House and the state legislatures' agents in the Senate."

The need for two powers to concur would, in turn, thwart the influence of special interests, and by satisfying two very different constituencies, would assure the enactment was for the greatest public good. Madison summed up the concept nicely in Federalist No 51:

> "In republican government, the legislative authority, necessarily predominate. The remedy for this inconveniency is, to divide the legislature into different branches; and to render them by different modes of election, and different principles of action, as little connected with each other, as the nature of their common functions and their common dependencies on the society, will admit."

The system as designed by the Framers was in place for a century and a quarter, from 1789 until 1913, when the Seventeenth Amendment was adopted. As originally designed, the Framers' system both protected federalism and ensured that relatively few benefits would be provided to special interests.

Cloudy Reasons

There is no agreement on why the system of electing Senators was changed through the enactment of the Seventeenth Amendment. But there is widespread agreement that the change was to the detriment of the states, and that it played a large part in dramatically changing the role of the national government.

Before the Seventeenth Amendment the federal government remained stable and small. Following the Amendment's adoption it has grown dramatically.

The conventional wisdom is that it was FDR's New Deal [President Franklin D. Roosevelt's reforms of the 1930s] that radically increased the size and power of federal government. But scholars make a convincing case that this conventional wisdom is wrong, and that instead, it was the Seventeenth Amendment (along with the Sixteenth Amendment, which created federal income tax and was also adopted in 1913) that was the driving force behind federal expansion.

The Amendment took a long time to come. It was not until 1820 that a resolution was introduced in the House of Representatives to amend the Constitution to provide for direct elections of Senators. And not until after the Civil War, in 1870, did calls for altering the system begin in earnest. But forty-three years passed before the change was actually made.

This lengthy passage of time clouds the causes that provoked the Amendment to be proposed and, finally, enacted. Nonetheless, scholars do have a number of theories to explain these developments.

George Mason University law professor Todd Zywicki has assembled an excellent analysis of the recent scholarship on the history of the Seventeenth Amendment, while also filling in its gaps. Zywicki finds, however, that received explanations are incomplete.

Two Main Theories Deficient

There have been two principal explanations for changing the Constitution to provide for direct election of Senators. Some see the Amendment as part of the Progressive Movement, which swept the nation in the late 1800s and early 1900s, giving us direct elections, recall, and referendums.

Others, however, believe the Amendment resulted from the problems the prior Constitutional system was creating in state legislatures, who under that system were charged with electing Senators. These problems ranged from charges of bribery to unbreakable deadlocks.

Deadlocks happened from time to time when, because of party imbalance, a legislature was unable to muster a majority (as necessary under the 1866 law that controlled) in favor of any person. The result was to leave the Senate seat empty and leave the state represented by only a single Senator, not the Constitutionally-mandated two.

Professor Zywicki basically demolishes both these explanations. He contends, first, that explaining the Seventeenth Amendment as part of the Progressive Movement is weak, at best. After all, nothing else from that movement (such as referendums and recalls) was adopted as part of the Constitution. He also points out that revisionist history indicates the Progressive Movement was not driven as much by efforts to aid the less fortunate as once was thought (and as it claimed)—so that direct democracy as an empowerment of the poor might not have been one of its true goals.

What about the "corruption and deadlock" explanation? Zywicki's analysis shows that, in fact, the corruption was nominal, and infrequent. In addition, he points out that the deadlock problem could have been easily solved by legislation that would have required only a plurality to elect a Senator—a far easier remedy than the burdensome process of amending the Constitution that led to the Seventeenth Amendment.

Fortunately, Professor Zywicki offers an explanation for the Amendment's enactment that makes much more sense. He contends that the true backers of the Seventeenth Amendment were special interests, which had had great difficulty influencing the system when state legislatures controlled the Senate. (Recall that it had been set up by the Framers precisely to thwart them.) They hoped direct elections would increase their control, since they would let them appeal directly to the electorate, as well as provide their essential political fuel—money.

This explanation troubles many. However, as Zywicki observes, "[al]though some might find this reality 'distasteful,' that does not make it any less accurate."

Should the Amendment Be Repealed?

Those unhappy with the Supreme Court's recent activism regarding federalism should consider joining those who believe the Seventeenth Amendment should be repealed. Rather than railing at life-tenured Justices who are inevitably going to chart their own courses, critics should focus instead on something they can affect, however difficult a repeal might be.

Repeal of the amendment would restore both federalism and bicameralism. It would also have a dramatic and positive effect on campaign spending. Senate races are currently among the most expensive. But if state legislatures were the focus of campaigns, more candidates might get more access with less money—decidedly a good thing.

Returning selection of Senators to state legislatures might be a cause that could attract both modern progressives and conservatives. For conservatives, obviously, it would be a return to the system envisioned by the Framers. For progressives—who now must appreciate that direct elections have only enhanced the ability of special interests to influence the process—returning to the diffusion of power inherent in federalism and bicameralism may seem an attractive alternative, or complement, to campaign finance reform.

Professor Zywicki likes this idea as well, but is probably right in finding repeal unlikely. He comments—and I believe he's got it right—"Absent a change of heart in the American populace and a better understanding of the beneficial role played by limitations on direct democracy, it is difficult to imagine a movement to repeal the Seventeenth Amendment."

The Seventeenth Amendment Destroyed Federalism in the United States

Zell Miller

On April 28, 2004, Georgia Democratic senator Zell Miller got up on the Senate floor to make a speech to go along with a bill he was proposing that would repeal the Seventeenth Amendment. Although he made reference to issues ranging from the possibility of terrorist attacks to allegedly overpowerful judges, Miller's main concern was that the Senate, as it then stood, was ineffective and failed to represent the interests of the states. He argued that the American republic was founded in such a way as to maintain a careful balance between the powers of the federal government and those of the independent states, a balance generally referred to by using the word federalism. *Because senators have to spend so much of their time raising money to ensure reelection, Miller charged, they are bound to those who provide the money rather than to the states they represent. One sign of this was the increasing number of mandates, or measures, passed by the federal government but requiring individual states to provide funding. According to Miller, repealing the Seventeenth Amendment would be key to restoring the federalism that America's founders intended. After earlier serving as the state's governor, Zell Miller served Georgia in the Senate from 2000 to 2005. He was initially appointed by Georgia governor Roy Barnes as a replacement for a standing senator who had passed away, but he won a special election soon after. He chose not to run again in 2004.*

Zell Miller, "Floor Statement on Repealing the 17th Amendment," Free Republic, April 28, 2004. Reproduced by permission.

We live in perilous times. The Leader of the Free World's power has become so neutered he cannot, even with the support of a majority of the Senate, appoint highly qualified individuals endorsed by the American Bar to a federal court.

He cannot conduct a war without being torn to shreds by partisans with their eyes set not on the defeat of our enemy but on the defeat of our President.

The U.S. Senate has become just one big, bad, ongoing joke, held hostage by special interests and so impotent an eighteen wheeler truck loaded with Viagra would do no good.

[Georgia politician] Andrew Young, one of America's most thoughtful men, recently took a long and serious look at a U.S. Senate race and after visiting Washington concluded that the Senate is composed of:

"A bunch of pompous old (folks) listening to people read statements they didn't even write and probably don't believe."

The House of Representatives, theoretically the closest of all the federal government to the people, cannot restrain its extravagant spending nor limit our spiraling debt.

And incumbents are so entrenched you might as well call off 80% of the House races. There are no contests.

Most of the laws of our land—at least, the most important and lasting ones—are made not by elected representatives of the people, but by unelected, unaccountable "legislators" in black robes who churn out volumes of case law and who hold their jobs for life [i.e., Supreme Court judges].

A half-dozen dirty bombs the size of a small suitcase planted around the country could bring this nation to its knees at any time. And yet we can't even build a fence along our border to keep out illegals because some nutty environmentalists say it will cause erosion.

Georgia senator Zell Miller argues that the direct election of senators shattered U.S. federalism. AP Images.

This government is in one helluva mess, and frankly my dear, very few up here give a damn.

It's not funny. It's sad. It's tragic and it can only get worse. Much worse. What this government needs is one of those extreme makeovers they have on television, and I'm not referring to some minor nose job or a little botox here and there.

Making the States Pay

Congressional Quarterly recently devoted an issue to the "Mandate Wars" with headlines blaring, "Unfunded Mandates Add to Woes, States Say," "Localities Get the Bill for Beefed-Up Security," "Transportation Money Comes With Strings," and "Medicaid Stuck in Funding Squabbles." Etcetera. Etcetera.

One would think that the much heralded "Unfunded Mandate Reform Act" of 1995 never passed. The National Conference of State Legislatures has set the unfunded mandate figure for the states at $33 billion for 2005. This, along with the budget problems they've been having for the last few years, has put states under the heel of a distant and unresponsive government. That's us!

And it gives the enthusiastic tax-raisers at the state level the very excuse they're looking for to dig deeper and deeper into the pockets of their taxpayers.

It's not a pretty picture. And no matter who you send to Washington—for the most part smart and decent people—it is not going to change much. The individuals are not so much at fault as the rotten and decaying foundation of what is no longer a republic.

It is the system that stinks. And it's only going to get worse because that perfect balance our brilliant Founding Fathers put in place in 1787 no longer exists. Perhaps then the answer is a return to the original thinking of those wisest of all men, and how they intended for this government to function.

Federalism, for all practical purposes, has become to this generation of leaders some vague philosophy of the past that is dead, dead, dead. It isn't even on life support. That line on the monitor went flat some time ago.

You see, the reformers of the early 1900's killed it dead and cremated the body when they allowed for the direct election of U.S. senators. Up until then, U.S. senators were chosen by state legislatures, as [James] Madison and [Alexander] Hamilton had so carefully crafted.

Problems Started with Amendment

Direct elections of senators, as good as that sounds, allowed Washington's special interests to call the shots, whether it's filling judicial vacancies or issuing regulations. The state governments aided in their own collective suicide by going along with the popular fad of the time.

Oh, today, it's heresy to even think about changing the system.

But can you imagine those dreadful unfunded mandates being put on the states or a homeland security bill being torpedoed by the unions if U.S. senators were still chosen by and responsible to the state legislatures?

Make no mistake about it. It is the special interest groups and their fundraising power that elect U.S. senators and then hold them in bondage forever. In the past five election cycles, senators have raised over $1.5 billion for their election contests, not counting all the soft money spent on their behalf in other ways. Few would believe it, but the daily business of the Senate is actually scheduled around fundraising.

The 17th Amendment was the death of the careful balance between state and federal governments. As designed by that brilliant and very practical group of Founding Fathers, the two governments would be in competition with each other and neither could abuse or threaten the other.

The election of U.S. senators by the state legislatures was the linchpin that guaranteed the interests of the states would be protected.

Today, state governments have to stand in line. They are just another one of many, many special interests that try to get senators to listen to them. And they are at an extreme disadvantage because they have no PAC [political action committee, a fundraising organization].

The great historian, Edward Gibbons, said of the decline of the Roman Empire, "The fine theory of a republic insensibly vanished."

That is exactly what happened in 1913 when the state legislatures, except for Utah and Delaware, rushed pell-mell to ratify the popular 17th Amendment and, by doing so, slashed their own throats and destroyed federalism forever. It was a victory for special interest tyranny and a blow to the power of state governments that would cripple them forever.

And so, instead of senators who thoughtfully make up their own minds, as they did during the Senate's greatest era of [Henry] Clay, [Daniel] Webster and [John] Calhoun [the 1830s and 1890s] we now have many senators who are mere cat's paws for the special interests. It is the Senate's sorriest time in its long, checkered and once-glorious history.

The Amendment Should Be Repealed

So, having now jumped off the Golden Gate Bridge of political reality, before I hit the water and go "splat," I have introduced a bill that would repeal the 17th Amendment. I use the word "would," not "will," because I know it doesn't stand a chance of getting even a single co-sponsor, much less a single vote beyond my own.

Abraham Lincoln, as a young man, made a speech in Springfield, Illinois, in which he called our founding principles "a fortress of strength," but warned that they "would grow more and more dim by the silent artillery of time."

A wise man, that Lincoln, who understood and predicted all too well the fate of our republic and our form of government. Too bad we didn't listen to him.

Repeal of the Seventeenth Amendment Will Not Improve the Senate

Lewis Gould

In the following selection, historian Lewis Gould comments on the bill introduced into the Senate in 2004 by Senator Zell Miller to repeal the Seventeenth Amendment. Miller's bill received vocal support from several quarters, among them Republican senatorial candidate from Illinois Alan Keyes, who ultimately lost the Illinois race to future president Barack Obama.

Gould returns to the historical context in which the Seventeenth Amendment was proposed and ratified to back up his claim that any repeal of the amendment would not result in an improvement of the Senate. He cites several examples of early twentieth-century senators who attempted to use their own or others' money to bribe state legislatures to vote them into office. It was such examples, Gould contends, that led to the direct election of senators in the first place. While the Senate could be less reliant on certain special interests and the necessity of campaign fund-raising, he admits, returning to the earlier system of senators chosen by state legislatures would result in ineffective changes. Lewis Gould is an emeritus professor of history at the University of Texas–Austin and a fellow at the university's Center for American History.

Alan Keyes, the Republican senatorial candidate in Illinois, has now joined Senator Zell Miller of Georgia and House Majority Leader Tom DeLay in calling for repeal of the Seventeenth Amendment to the Constitution, the one that provides for the direct election of United States senators. Senator Miller,

Lewis Gould, "Alan Keyes' Daffy Idea to Repeal the 17th Amendment," History News Network, August 23, 2004. Reproduced by permission.

who has introduced his own amendment to repeal the Seventeenth, contends that the direct election of senators "was the death of the careful balance between state and federal governments." Once the Senate was the province of members "who thoughtfully make up their own minds, as they did during the Senate's greatest era of Clay, Webster, and Calhoun." Now senators, in Miller's view, "are mere cat's paws for the special interests." Miller favors returning the right to elect senators to the state legislatures who had that job until the Seventeenth Amendment was ratified in 1913. Keyes agrees since it seems likely that the Illinois electorate is not going to prove receptive to his bid for that state's open Senate seat. Before this flawed idea gets any traction, it would be well to recall the historical circumstances that led to the adoption of the direct election amendment in the first place.

Why did Americans in the Progressive Era endorse this change in the nation's fundamental law? Put aside the senatorial giants that Miller mentions—John C. Calhoun, Daniel Webster, and Henry Clay. Consider three lesser known figures in the history of the upper house—J. Edward Addicks, William A. Clark, and William Lorimer. Few history books devote more than a line or two to these three obscure gentlemen, but they were important players in the reason why the Seventeenth Amendment came into being.

Context of the Seventeenth Amendment

By 1900 complaints about the way that United States senators were elected filled the press of the day. "The legislative system of electing Senators has broken down," wrote a commentator in the [magazine] *Arena* in 1905. Critics cited the senators who had recently been indicted and convicted of crimes, Joseph R. Burton of Kansas and John Mitchell of Oregon. Other senators such as Chauncey Depew of New York had been found to be on the payroll of corporations. There was in the

Senate the general presence, as the [magazine the] *Nation* put it, of "those whose corruption or surrender to corporate interests has too long stained the reputation of a great legislative body." Politicians associated with the Progressive Movement, such as William E. Borah of Idaho and Joseph L. Bristow of Kansas, argued that direct election represented a forward step toward cleaner politics when corruptible state legislatures gave way to the people.

Now to those three obscure men. William A. Clark was a wealthy silver miner from Montana whom the legislature in that state sent to the Senate in 1899. Subsequent investigation determined that he had spent more than $140,000 of his money bribing lawmakers in the legislature. After resigning his seat in early 1900, he was returned to the Senate by the Montana legislature under less sordid conditions. J. Edward Addicks was a millionaire from Pennsylvania who tried to buy himself a Senate seat from Delaware in the 1890s and early 1900s. Spreading his cash around, he put the state into a political turmoil that left it without one of its senators for several years. Finally, Senator William Lorimer received a majority of the votes from the Illinois legislature in 1909. Later revelations disclosed that bribery of some legislators had been a key part of Lorimer's victory. The senator himself was not involved with the illegal acts, but the specter of "Lorimerism" convinced many citizens that legislatures were not the proper vehicles for selecting United States senators. In 1912 Lorimer was expelled from the Senate. By then the direct election of senators had become a constitutional amendment and was on its way to ratification.

Returning to the Past Is Not the Answer

The Seventeenth Amendment did not bring the new political morality to the Senate that its advocates had forecast. Many problems of campaign finance, corrupted elections, and the power of special interests remain to plague the Senate chamber. But a resolution of those issues will not occur by returning to a fancied golden age of senatorial excellence before the Seventeenth Amendment came on the scene. State legislatures are not the answer to improving the Senate any more than they were in 1900. Such a reversion might have the effect of reducing campaign expenses since the cost of influencing several dozen state lawmakers would be well below the current outlay for running a statewide election. Yet it is laughable, in light of the historical experience of a century ago, to suggest that a return to a system so susceptible to corruption, logrolling [trading favors], and the flouting of public opinion would be any kind of improvement over the present state of affairs. The contemporary problems of the Senate need to be addressed. Relying on the undemocratic methods that came before the Seventeenth Amendment provides no way to embark on the salutary process of reforming the Senate.

The Seventeenth Amendment Should Be Changed to Prevent State Governors from Appointing Senators

Russ Feingold

The 2008 election of Barack Obama and Joe Biden as U.S. president and vice president left their respective Illinois and Delaware Senate seats open. Two more Senate vacancies occurred once Obama selected his cabinet, because he chose Senator Hillary Rodham Clinton of New York as secretary of state and Senator Ken Salazar of Colorado as secretary of the interior. Pending elections, those four seats were to be filled by replacements chosen by the governors of Illinois, Delaware, New York, and Colorado.

In the following viewpoint, Wisconsin senator Russ Feingold argues that special elections should be held for senatorial replacements, and he introduces a new constitutional amendment to ensure this procedure. Special elections, he claims, would be a closer reflection of the true spirit of the Seventeenth Amendment, which was passed on the principle that it would be a state's voters, not their governors, who would choose their senators. He suggests that a new amendment, passed on a national level, would be preferable to seeking procedural changes in each of the fifty states, where most governors retained the ability to appoint senatorial replacements in between elections. Democrat Russ Feingold has served Wisconsin in the Senate since 1993.

Our founding fathers did a remarkable job in drafting the United States Constitution and the Bill of Rights. Their work was so superb that in the 217 years since the ratification

Russ Feingold, "Statement of Senator Russ Feingold on Introduction of a Constitutional Amendment Concerning Senate Vacancies," www.feingold.senate.gov, January 29, 2009.

of the Bill of Rights, the Constitution has only been amended 17 times. But every so often, a situation arises that so clearly exposes a flaw in our constitutional structure that it requires a constitutional remedy.

Over the past several months, our country has witnessed multiple controversies surrounding appointments to vacant Senate seats by governors. The vacancies in Illinois and New York have made for riveting political theater, but lost in the seemingly endless string of press conferences and surprise revelations is the basic fact that the citizens of these states have had no say in who should represent them in the Senate. The same is true of the recent selections in Delaware and Colorado. That is why I will introduce today a constitutional amendment to end gubernatorial appointments to the U.S. Senate and require special elections to fill these vacancies, as is currently required for House vacancies. I am pleased that the recently elected Senator from Alaska, Senator [Mark] Begich, and the distinguished senior Senator from Arizona, Senator [John] McCain, have agreed to be original cosponsors of the amendment.

I do not make this proposal lightly. In fact, I have opposed dozens of constitutional amendments during my time in the Senate, particularly those that would have interfered with the Bill of Rights. The Constitution should not be treated like a rough draft. Constitutional amendments should be considered only when a statutory remedy to a problem is not available, and when the impact of the issue at hand on the structure of our government, the safety, welfare, or freedoms of our citizens, or the survival of our democratic republic is so significant that an amendment is warranted. I believe this is such a case.

Good Reasons for Adoption

In 1913, the citizens of this country, acting through their elected state legislatures, ratified the 17th Amendment to the

Constitution. Our esteemed colleague Sen. [Robert] Byrd, in Chapter 21 of his remarkable history of the United States Senate, lays out in fascinating detail the lengthy struggle to obtain for the citizens of this country the right to elect their Senators. The original Constitution, as we all know, gave state legislatures the right to choose the Senators for their states. While the first proposal to amend the Constitution to require the direct election of Senators was introduced in the House in 1826, the effort only really picked up steam after the Civil War.

As Sen. Byrd recounts: "In the post-Civil War period, state legislatures became increasingly subject to intimidation and bribery in the selection of Senators." Nine cases of bribery came before the Senate between 1866 and 1906. And between 1891 and 1905, the state legislatures from 20 different states deadlocked 45 times when trying to pick a Senator. At one point, a Senate seat from Delaware remained vacant for four years because of deadlocks.

The political theater occasioned by these Senate appointment fights dwarfs even the extraordinary events we have witnessed in recent months. Sen. Byrd quotes from an account by the historian George Haynes about efforts to select a Senator in Missouri in 1905:

> Lest the hour of adjournment should come before an election was secured, an attempt was made to stop the clock upon the wall of the assembly chamber. Democrats tried to prevent its being tampered with; and when certain Republicans brought forward a ladder, it was seized and thrown out of the window. A fist-fight followed, in which many were involved. Desks were torn from the floor and a fusillade of books began. The glass of the clock-front was broken, but the pendulum still persisted in swinging until, in the midst of a yelling mob, one member began throwing ink bottles at the clock, and finally succeeded in breaking the pendulum. On a motion to adjourn, arose the wildest disorder. The presiding officers of both houses mounted the speaker's

desk, and, by shouting and waving their arms, tried to quiet the mob. Finally, they succeeded in securing some semblance of order.

Popular sentiment for direct election of Senators slowly grew in response to events like these. Some states held popular referenda on who should be Senator and attempted to require their legislatures to select the winners of those votes. More and more Senators were chosen in such processes, leading to more support in the Senate for a constitutional amendment. Congress finally acted in 1911 and 1912. There was high drama in the Senate as Vice President James Schoolcraft Sherman broke a tie on a crucial substitute amendment offered by Senator Joseph Bristow of Kansas during Senate consideration of the joint resolution. A few days of parliamentary wrangling ensued over whether the Vice President's tie breaking role in the Senate extends to such situations, and that precedent still stands today. In May 1912, an impasse of almost a year was broken and the House receded to the Senate version of the amendment, allowing it to be sent to the states for ratification. Less than a year later, on April 8, 1913, Connecticut became the 36th state to ratify the amendment, and it became the 17th Amendment to the Constitution.

People Must Elect Their Representatives

I recount this summary of the history of the 17th Amendment, and again, I commend to my colleagues Sen. Byrd's chapter on the subject, first to make the point that even though it seems obvious to us that the Senate should be elected by the people, the struggle for that right was not easy or fast. But the cause was just and in the end the call for direct elections was too strong to be ignored. I believe the same result will occur here. It may take time, but in the end, I am confident that the principle that people must elect their representatives will prevail.

Second, this history shows that the public's disgust with the corruption, bribery, and political chicanery that resulted from having Senators chosen by state legislatures was a big motivation for passing the amendment. Gubernatorial appointments pose the same dangers, and demand the same solution—direct elections.

Finally, the history indicates that the proviso in the 17th amendment permitting gubernatorial appointments to fill temporary vacancies was not the subject of extensive debate in the Congress. The proviso originated in the substitute amendment offered by Senator Bristow. The Bristow substitute was designed, its sponsor explained, to "make the least possible change in the Constitution to accomplish the purposes desired; that is the election of Senators by popular vote." Most significantly, it deleted a provision in the resolution as originally introduced that year that would have amended Article I, section 4 of the Constitution to remove Congress's supervisory authority to make or alter regulations concerning the time and manner of Senate elections.

The proviso, explained Sen. Bristow, "is practically the same provision which now exists in the case of such a vacancy. The governor of the State may appoint a Senator until the legislature elects." Although significant debate over other provisions in the Bristow amendment is found in the Record before the climactic tie vote, which was broken by the Vice President, there seems to have been no further discussion of the proviso.

Thus, it appears that the proviso was simply derived from the original constitutional provision in Article I, Section 3, which gave the power to choose Senators to the state legislatures, but allowed governors to appoint temporary replacements when the legislatures were not in session. It was unremarkable at the time of the 17th Amendment to allow governors to have the same temporary replacement power once direct elections were required. That would explain the apparent lack of debate on the question. The long and contentious debate over the amendment was dominated by much more basic issues, such as whether the people should elect their Senators at all, and whether Congress should also amend the "time, place, or manner clause" of Article I, section 4.

Nearly 100 years later, that proviso has allowed a total of 184 Senators to be appointed by governors, and we have a situation in today's Senate where the people of four states, comprising over 12 percent of the entire population of the country, will be represented for the next two years by someone they did not elect. It is very hard to imagine that the Congress that passed the 17th Amendment and the states that ratified it would have been comfortable with such an outcome. Indeed, some argue that the intent of the 17th Amendment was that temporary appointments to fill early vacancies should last only until a special election can be scheduled, rather than for an entire two-year Congress until the next general election. A number of states have adopted that approach, but many have not.

That is not to say that the people appointed to Senate seats are not capable of serving, or will not do so honorably. I have no reason to question the fitness for office of any of the most recent appointees, and I look forward to working with them. But those who want to be a U.S. Senator should have to make their case to the people whom they want to represent, not just the occupant of the governor's mansion. And the voters should choose them in the time-honored way that they choose the rest of the Congress of the United States.

Fulfilling the Seventeenth Amendment

I want to make it clear that this proposal is not simply a response to these latest cases that have been in the news over the past few months. These cases have simply confirmed my longstanding view that Senate appointments by state governors are an unfortunate relic of the pre-17th Amendment era, when state legislatures elected U.S. Senators. Direct election of Senators was championed by the great progressive Bob La Follette, who served as Wisconsin's Governor and a U.S. Senator. Indeed, my state of Wisconsin is now one of only four states (Oregon, Massachusetts, and Alaska are the others) that clearly require a special election to fill a Senate vacancy in all circumstances.

The vast majority of states still rely on the appointment system, while retaining the right to require direct elections, as the Massachusetts legislature and the voters of Alaska have done in recent years. But changing this system state by state would be a long and difficult process, even more difficult than the ratification of a constitutional amendment, particularly since Governors have the power to veto state statutes that would take this power away from them. Furthermore, the burden should not be on Americans to pass legislation in their states protecting their fundamental voting rights—the right to elect one's representatives is a bedrock principle and should be reaffirmed in the nation's ruling charter.

We need to finish the job started by La Follette and other reformers nearly a century ago. Nobody can represent the people in the House of Representatives without the approval of the voters. The same should be true for the Senate.

Addressing Objections

In the several days since I announced my intention to introduce this amendment, I have heard a number of arguments raised against it. I would like to briefly address them. First of all, some suggest this amendment is an overreaction to the headlines of the day. But there are several precedents for amending the provisions of the Constitution that relate to the structure of government based on specific events. The 22nd Amendment, limiting the presidency to two terms, passed in 1951 in response to President Franklin D. Roosevelt's four-term presidency. And the 25th Amendment, revising presidential succession, was passed in 1967 in response to confusion that occurred after the assassination of President [John F.] Kennedy. If events demonstrate that there is a problem with our government structure, sooner or later we must take steps to address those problems. There is no better time to do that than when the effects of the structural flaw are most evident and most prominently part of the public debate.

Another objection I have heard to this proposal is the potential financial burden on the states that must pay for special elections. As someone with a reputation for fiscal discipline, I always consider a proposal's impact on the taxpayer. But the cost to our democracy of continuing the anachronism of gubernatorial Senate appointments is far greater than the cost of infrequent special elections. And weighing the costs associated with the most basic tenet of our democracy—the election of the government by the governed—sets us on a dangerous path. Besides, the Constitution already requires special elections when a House seat becomes vacant, a far more frequent occurrence since there are so many more Representatives than Senators. I find the cost argument wholly unconvincing.

Another argument I have heard is that special elections garner very low turnouts, or favor wealthy or well known candidates. They are not particularly democratic, the argument goes. And that may very well be true. But they are a whole lot more democratic than the election held inside the mind of one decisionmaker—the governor. Special elections may not be ideal, but they are elections, and every voter has the opportunity to participate. As Winston Churchill said, "It has been said that democracy is the worst form of government except all the others that have been tried."

I have also heard the argument that the candidates for the special election will be selected by party bosses because there won't be time for a primary. That is simply not true. Under this amendment, each state can decide how to set up its special elections. My home state of Wisconsin provides for a special election within about 10 weeks of the vacancy, with a primary one month earlier. It's a compressed schedule to be sure, because the state doesn't want to be without representation for too long. But it can be done. I would hope that most states would want to hold primaries, but the point of this amendment is to make clear that only Senators who have been elected by the people can serve, not to micromanage how the states want to implement that requirement.

I believe the core issue here is whether we are going to have a government that is as representative of and responsive to the people as possible. The time to require special elections to fill Senate vacancies has come. Congress should act quickly on this proposal, and send it to the states for ratification.

The Seventeenth Amendment Should Not Be Changed but Should Be Repealed Altogether

George Will

In the following selection, conservative columnist George Will questions Senator Russ Feingold's desire to alter the U.S. Constitution so that special elections, not state governors, choose replacements for senators who enter other offices, retire, or pass away. Will believes that Feingold's proposed amendment would be yet another attack on the federalism that America's founders initially intended or, in other words, a reduction of the rights and freedoms of individual states and an increase in the scope and power of the national government.

To Will's mind, the Seventeenth Amendment itself was a mistake in that it lessened the ability of the states to form and influence the national government. Nor did it improve the Senate's quality; he cites the fact that it was state legislatures that chose such senatorial giants as Henry Clay, Daniel Webster, and John Calhoun in the pre–Civil War era. Meanwhile, direct elections resulted in such dubious figures as Joe McCarthy, a senator from Feingold's own state of Wisconsin and the leader of the Senate's anti-Communist witchhunt of the 1950s. Pulitzer Prize–winning columnist George Will has written regularly for both the Washington Post *and* Newsweek *since the 1970s. He also works as a political analyst for the ABC television network.*

A simple apology would have sufficed. Instead, Sen. Russ Feingold has decided to follow his McCain-Feingold[1] evisceration of the First Amendment with Feingold-McCain, more vandalism against the Constitution.

1. The 2002 McCain-Feingold Act regulated campaign financing.

George Will, "Senator Feingold's Constitution," *The Washington Post*, February 22, 2009. Reprinted with permission.

The Wisconsin Democrat, who is steeped in his state's progressive tradition, says, as would-be amenders of the Constitution often do, that he is reluctant to tamper with the document but tamper he must because the threat to the public weal is immense: Some governors have recently behaved badly in appointing people to fill U.S. Senate vacancies. Feingold's solution, of which [Arizona senator] John McCain is a co-sponsor, is to amend the 17th Amendment. It would be better to repeal it.

The Framers established election of senators by state legislators, under which system the nation got the Great Triumvirate (Henry Clay, Daniel Webster and John Calhoun) and thrived. In 1913, progressives, believing that more, and more direct, democracy is always wonderful, got the 17th Amendment ratified. It stipulates popular election of senators, under which system Wisconsin has elected, among others, Joe McCarthy, as well as Feingold.

The 17th Amendment says that when Senate vacancies occur, "the executive authority" of the affected state "shall issue writs of election to fill such vacancies: Provided, That the legislature of any State may empower the executive thereof to make temporary appointments until the people fill the vacancies by election as the legislature may direct."

Feingold's amendment says:

"No person shall be a Senator from a State unless such person has been elected by the people thereof. When vacancies happen in the representation of any State in the Senate, the executive authority of such state shall issue writs of election to fill such vacancies."

Senate and House Are Different

Feingold says that mandating election of replacement senators is necessary to make the Senate as "responsive to the people as possible." Well. The House, directly elected and with two-year terms, was designed for responsiveness. The Senate, indirectly elected and with six-year terms, was to be more deliberative than responsive.

Furthermore, grounding the Senate in state legislatures served the structure of federalism. Giving the states an important role in determining the composition of the federal government gave the states power to resist what has happened since 1913—the progressive (in two senses) reduction of the states to administrative extensions of the federal government.

Severing senators from state legislatures, which could monitor and even instruct them, made them more susceptible to influence by nationally organized interest groups based in Washington. Many of those groups, who preferred one-stop shopping in Washington to currying favors in all the state capitals, campaigned for the 17th Amendment. So did urban political machines, which were then organizing an uninformed electorate swollen by immigrants. Alliances between such interests and senators led to a lengthening of the senators' tenures.

Checks and Balances Removed

The Framers gave the three political components of the federal government (the House, Senate and presidency) different electors (the people, the state legislatures and the electoral college as originally intended) to reinforce the principle of separation of powers, by which government is checked and balanced.

Although liberals give lip service to "diversity," they often treat federalism as an annoying impediment to their drive for uniformity. Feingold, who is proud that Wisconsin is one of only four states that clearly require special elections of replacement senators in all circumstances, wants to impose Wisconsin's preference on the other 46. Yes, he acknowledges, they could each choose to pass laws like Wisconsin's, but doing this "state by state would be a long and difficult process." Pluralism is so tediously time-consuming.

Irony alert: Feingold's amendment requiring elections to fill Senate vacancies will owe any traction it gains to Senate Democrats' opposition to an election to choose a replacement for Barack Obama. That opposition led to the ongoing Blagojevich-Burris fiasco.[2]

By restricting the financing of political advocacy, the McCain-Feingold speech-rationing law empowers the government to regulate the quantity, timing and content of political speech. Thanks to Feingold, McCain and others, the First Amendment now, in effect, reads: "Congress shall make no law . . . abridging the freedom of speech *unless it really, really wants to in order to guarantee that there will be only as much speech about the government as the government considers appropriate, and at times the government approves.*"

Now Feingold proposes to traduce federalism and nudge the Senate still further away from the nature and function the Framers favored. He is, as the saying goes, an unapologetic progressive, but one with more and more for which to apologize.

---

2. Illinois governor Rod Blagojevich was indicted on corruption charges for asking for favors in exchange for appointing a new senator to fill Obama's seat. He appointed Roland Burris.

The Seventeenth Amendment Is an Improvement on the Alternatives

Publius

In the following selection, a blogger who calls himself Publius (Latin for "the Public") comments on writer George Will's criticism of the proposal of Senator Russ Feingold that a new constitutional amendment ensure that senatorial replacements be directly elected rather than chosen by governors. Publius disagrees with Will's sense that senators chosen by state legislatures, as they were before the Seventeenth Amendment was ratified, or by state governors, as they still commonly are, results in a wiser, better Senate than one chosen by voters through direct democracy. He asserts that leaving the choice to state legislatures or governors opens up the process to corruption, citing the example of former Illinois governor Rod Blagojevich, or Blago. Blagojevich was impeached by a unanimous vote of the Illinois State Senate in January 2009 after allegedly requesting bribes in exchange for choosing the replacement for newly elected president and former senator Barack Obama. Indeed, such examples of "pay for play" were what helped inspire the Seventeenth Amendment in the first place, Publius argues. To Publius, leaving senatorial choices to the public, while not perfect, is a much better option. According to the blog for which he writes, Obsidian Wings, Publius is a professor of law in Texas.

If I were the snarking type, I might respond to George Will's latest [column titled "Senator Feingold's Constitution," *Washington Post*, February 22, 2009,] by saying something like "Shorter George Will—directly electing Senators harms America." But that's not my style, so I'll try to address the merits.

Publius (John Blevins), "Repeal the 17th Amendment?" Obsidian Wings, February 22, 2009. Reproduced by permission of the author.

"Sell Obama's Senate seat and pocket the money!" by Ed Fischer. www.CartoonStock
.com.

In criticizing Feingold's proposed amendment to require
special elections for Senate vacancies, Will argues that the entire 17th Amendment should be repealed. Instead, he would
prefer that state legislatures still appointed Senators. Letting
the rabble directly elect Senators violates the framers' design
and harms federalism.

What's interesting about Will's position is how it adopts
one extremely old-school version of conservative thought,
while ignoring another entirely. Will is an old-school conservative in that he hasn't fully embraced democracy. ("In 1913,
progressives, believing that more, and more direct, democracy
is always wonderful . . .")

In theory, Will's argument sounds plausible. It certainly
sounds nice to picture state legislatures as wise, deliberative
bodies, weighing their appointments carefully—unlike how
the rabble makes its decisions. But that's not how legislative
appointments would work—indeed, that's not how they used

to work. The problem is that Will is ignoring an even more fundamental conservative insight—namely, that people are bad.

Inviting Corruption

The point of requiring elections is not because people always make wise decisions. The point is that it's the most legitimate method and the single-best protection against corruption.

The problem with governor appointments is a structural one—one that goes beyond the individual moral failings of people like Blago [impeached Illinois governor Rod Blagojevich]. We currently have a vacancy appointment system in which the Blagos of the world have incentives to do funny business (demanding money; extracting concessions, etc.). As long as the incentives are there, future Blagos will inevitably reappear.

Providing state legislatures this authority raises all the same problems. In appointing Senators, state legislators would have all kinds of incentives to engage in corruption in exchange for a Senate appointment. And because those incentives are there—and because we must assume people will be bad when thinking of constitutional structure—corruption would inevitably occur.

Better to let us poor members of the rabble decide. Yes, state legislatures may be harder to bribe than a single governor. But it's still infinitely easier than trying to bribe the public as a whole.

CONSTITUTIONAL
AMENDMENTS
BEYOND THE BILL OF RIGHTS

CHAPTER 3

The Seventeenth Amendment in Contemporary America

The Seventeenth Amendment Ensures That Senators Are Directly Elected

Constitutional Accountability Center

The following selection is by the Constitutional Accountability Center, a progressive think tank and action center. It was written less than a week after the elections of November 2008. These elections resulted in some senate races that were so close they remained undecided for days (and, in one case, months) after the votes were cast. In Alaska, longtime Republican senator Ted Stevens faced a challenge from Democrat Mark Begich, who finally prevailed. In Oregon, Democrat Jeff Merkley was pronounced the winner over incumbent Republican Gordon Smith on November 6, although Smith did not concede for some days afterward. In Georgia, Republican Saxby Chambliss won a December 2 runoff election (held because neither candidate had received more than 50 percent of the vote in the initial contest) against Democratic challenger Jim Martin. The closest and most contentious election, meanwhile, was in Minnesota. There, incumbent Republican Norm Coleman faced a stiff challenge from writer, comedian, and political newcomer Al Franken. Franken was finally declared the winner on June 30, 2009, by the state supreme court. The selection points out that because of the Seventeenth Amendment, guaranteeing popular election of senators, the votes would be counted carefully and fully.

Three Senate races from last Tuesday's election [November 4, 2008,] remain undecided today [November 10, 2008], with one race (Minnesota's) down to only a 204-vote margin. In light of the impact each and every vote has in these races,

Elizabeth Wydra and Hannah McCrea, "Thanks to the 17th Amendment, Every Vote Will Count in Undecided Senate Races," Constitutional Accountability Center (www.theusconstitution.org), November 10, 2008. Reproduced by permission.

it bears remembering that the principle of "one person, one vote" has only applied in the election of U.S. Senators since the progressive constitutional reforms of the early 20th century.

Under the original Constitution, U.S. Senators were chosen not by the people, but by state legislators. Article 1, Section 3 of the Constitution provides that "the Senate of the United States shall be composed of two Senators from each state, chosen by the legislature thereof, for six years; and each Senator shall have one vote." The 17th Amendment, ratified in 1913, was part of a wave of progressive constitutional reforms that sought to make the Constitution, and our nation, more democratic. It gave Americans the right to vote directly for their Senators, thereby strengthening the link between citizens and the federal government. In addition to the 17th Amendment, the first half of the 20th century saw the ratification of two other important progressive amendments: the 16th Amendment, also ratified in 1913, which allowed for a truly progressive federal income tax, and the 19th Amendment, ratified in 1920, which extended the vote to women.

The Seventeenth Amendment in Action

As Yale Law Professor Akhil Reed Amar writes in *America's Constitution: A Biography*, the 17th Amendment had the effect of improving legislative accountability at both the state and federal levels. State legislators, for example, were now spared the time-consuming, and often corrupting, process of being quietly lobbied by individuals interested in becoming senators. And directly-elected senators found it easier to support policies that served citizens but that may not have been so popular among state legislators, thereby making the federal government more directly responsive to the electorate.

This week, all Americans should be celebrating this shift toward direct popular election of the Senate. As the recounts and runoffs in Georgia, Alaska, and Minnesota get under way, the importance of each and every vote in Senate races will be on full display, just as is our Constitution's history as an increasingly inclusionary, and fundamentally progressive, document.

Politicians Should Not Try to Circumvent the Intent of the Seventeenth Amendment

Michael Collins

The aftermath of the 2008 elections created a pair of notable test cases related to the Seventeenth Amendment's requirement that senators be directly elected. In the following selection, writer and elections watchdog Michael Collins, who maintains a Web site called electionfraudnews.com, examines these two cases and the ways in which, he alleges, both Democrats and Republicans wanted to manipulate election rules in order to ensure a desired outcome.

In Minnesota, the race between Democrat Al Franken and Republican Norm Coleman was so close—fewer than 230 votes divided the two—that it triggered an automatic recount of the votes under Minnesota state law. Even though the recount resulted in another close race, Franken maintained a small lead. Collins hoped that Minnesota election officials would verify these results and that the state's governor, Republican Tim Pawlenty, would certify the election and send Franken to the Senate. As it happened, Coleman mounted legal challenges that were not rejected until June 30, 2009, leaving Minnesota short one senator for nearly six months.

In Illinois, Governor Rod Blagojevich maintained the ability under state law to appoint a replacement to serve out the remaining two years of newly elected president Barack Obama's Senate term. Blagojevich, however, was indicted on corruption charges for allegedly asking for bribes in return for naming a replacement senator. The governor was ultimately removed from office by the Illinois state legislature but not before he had named Roland Burris to replace Obama.

Michael Collins, "Franken, Burris, and the U.S. Senate: Try Following the Rules," *American Politics Journal*, January 4, 2009. Reproduced by permission.

Collins vehemently asks why, in both cases, opponents to Franken and Blagojevich/Burris wanted to circumvent standing laws and why Franken's election was questioned by Republican senators outside of Minnesota when it was conducted in full accord with the state's election rules. He also wonders why Illinois Democratic senator Dick Durbin wanted a special election to replace Obama, seeing that even with the cloud over Blagojevich's head, state procedures for senatorial replacements were followed.

We've seen what happens when people don't follow the letter and intent of important laws, particularly those where there is a general consensus and an absence of moral ambiguity. Consider our history from the implosion of Enron [energy company that went bankrupt in 2001 after an accounting scandal] through the stock market collapse [of 2008]. This extreme damage was enabled by the deliberate defiance, evasion, and perversion of rules and laws, all in the service of personal gain for a very few. Citizens lost $6 trillion in that episode of lawlessness.

President [George W.] Bush and his administration consistently broke the laws of the United States by illegally tapping phones and emails, "selling" the Iraq invasion based on outright lies, and, in the case of six cabinet officials, participating in the "choreography" of torture sessions. All of them found the Constitution a nuisance and rendered it meaningless by their actions. The cost of these violations is incalculable.

Defiance of National Laws

A government gains legitimacy through the ascent to shared rules and laws by the vast majority of citizens. No government can retain legitimacy, however, when the legislature fails to enforce and live by the very laws that they are sworn to protect.

Democrats and Republicans are now unified along party lines in their defiance of the laws. Is this the new national unity we've been hearing about?

Yet this is exactly what is happening in the cases of the legally appointed Senator from Illinois, Roland Burris, and the soon to be certified winner of the Minnesota senatorial election, Al Franken. Republicans are threatening to delay the seating of Franken, even when he's certified the winner of the Minnesota Senate seat. Senate Democrats all signed a letter of implied threat to the governor of Illinois regarding his selection of Roland Burris as the U.S. Senator from Illinois.

The final vote count for Franken shows him winning by a narrow margin. The same elections system that conducted the recount will recommend and likely receive certification of the election quickly by the authorized state authority.

Burris was appointed by Gov. Rod Blagojevich (D-IL) according to the laws of Illinois. There's no provision that says a governor can't make a selection if he's been indicted for any crime. The Illinois Supreme Court refused to remove the governor when the request was made by the State Attorney General. The Illinois legislature could have impeached him but it didn't. He is still the governor of Illinois. [Blagojevich was later impeached and removed from office.]

Senate objections to Franken and Burris show that the United States Senate has thrown out the rule book and is ignoring established law when it comes to plans for the "presumptive" Senator from Minnesota, Al Franken, and the legally appointed Senator from Illinois, Roland Burris.

The Laws Were Followed

A candidate or appointee only has three requirements to be a legitimate Senator.

Article I, Section 3 of the Constitution states: "No Person shall be a Senator who shall not have attained to the Age of thirty Years, and been nine Years a Citizen of the United States, and who shall not, when elected, be an Inhabitant of that State for which he shall be chosen."

Both Al Franken and Roland Burris pass muster for these requirements.

The XVII Amendment to the U.S. Constitution outlines the popular election of Senators and the authority and procedures required to replace them in case they leave for some reason.

This amendment provided for the popular election of Senators. This is so simple. Elected and appointed Senators should be immune from the actions by any judicial authority unless there are violations of state or federal law in the process of appointments.

But the Senate has one slim provision that can be invoked in the case of a real controversy or a contrived political event.

Article I, Section 5 states that: "Each House shall be the judge of the elections, returns and qualifications of its own members."

This provides the Senate with the option of rejecting a prospective member. In point of fact, there have been more than a few challenges to elections, mostly in the House. No Senator has ever been denied a seat as a result of Article I, Section 5.

Seat Franken as Senator

Al Franken lost the initial vote count by less than one half of one percent of the total vote. That qualified him for an automatic recount. Minnesota election law clearly specifies a recount process and even states that the recount vote will be different than the initial reported election result: [According to Minnesota officials,] "Once the recount is over, the state elections board certifies the election. The election is over at the point the results are certified."

"The final results as modified, if necessary, by the recount are considered the final results of the election and are certified as final by the canvassing board."

The Uptake.Org reported [in early January 2009] that final recounting is finished and Franken has a 225 vote lead. The Minnesota Secretary of State commented at a post recount conference that any election contest challenging the recount would be futile. He praised the openness and fairness of the recount. At a post recount press conference, [Republican incumbent] Norm Coleman's representatives said they'd recommend a challenge in the form of a Minnesota election contest but indicated that the former Senator (his term expired Jan. 3 at noon) had not reached a decision.

The recount proceeded in an open and transparent way. Results were reported by the Secretary of State and in the state's major newspapers daily. Controversies between the campaigns were handled by the appropriate courts and decisions were made in a very timely fashion.

Franken followed every single rule. He did what many candidates fail to do. He fought for the right of Minnesota voters to have their ballots counted and the right of all citizens of that state to have a Senator elected by a majority of the voters. Norm Coleman, the initial winner, chided Franken for taking the option of a mandatory recount. Franken didn't back down or complain. He simply followed the rules and will very likely be certified as winner and therefore U.S. Senator from Minnesota.

Making Up Rules Is Absurd

But Republicans are now talking about making up their own rules. They don't want Franken seated until the conclusion of an anticipated appeal of the election through an "election contest." Sen. John Cornyn (R-TX), head of the Republican Senate Campaign Committee, threatened "chaos" if the Democrats tried "to jam this issue through the Senate and seat a senator who has not been determined to be the winner of the election"

Wait a minute! The canvassing board is the duly impaneled body that "determines" the "winner" of the election. . . . Does this mean that any certified winner of a Senate race can be denied his seat by a legal challenge of the final decision?

It's absurd. Cornyn can object all he wants. The rules are clear. Franken should be seated if certified the winner, as anticipated. There is no valid precedent in any of the election contests in the past to deny him that seat. . . .

If Coleman pursues a post certification election contest, the Minnesota canvassing board certification becomes "provisional" by state law indicating that a contest is under way. It may take three months to resolve the election contest. The citizens of Minnesota will be denied representation should the Senate refuse to seat the declared winner after certification. [A contest was pursued and the Minnesota Supreme Court declared Franken the winner on June 30, 2009.]

Seat Roland Burris Now

Roland Burris, the former Illinois Attorney General and Comptroller, was selected by indicted Governor Rod Blagojevich to fill the term of President elect Barrack Obama. The day after the governor's arrest, Illinois senior Senator, Richard Durbin (D-IL), appealed to Blagojevich to call for a special election rather than make an appointment to fill President-elect Obama's vacated Senate seat.

> "Please understand that should you decide to ignore the request of the Senate Democratic Caucus and make an appointment we would be forced to exercise our Constitutional authority under Article I, Section 5, to determine whether such a person should be seated."

> "We do not prejudge the outcome of the criminal charges against you or question your constitutional right to contest those charges. But for the good of the Senate and our nation, we implore you to refrain from making an appointment to the Senate."

Signed by the entire Senate Democratic leadership and all members of the Democratic Caucus.

In the first paragraph above, Sen. Durbin says that the Democratic Caucus "would be forced to exercise [its] Constitutional authority" to review the appointment. This is a reference to Article I, Section 5 above. The "Senate Democratic Caucus" has no authority under the United States Constitution. It isn't even mentioned [in the Constitution]. The Senate does have the authority to "be the Judge of the Elections, Returns and Qualifications of its own Members." But no Senator or group of Senators is "forced" to do this.

Doesn't this sound like an implied threat? "We want a special election not an appointment by you, Rod. Go right ahead and we'll invoke that section of Article I, Section 5 on Qualifications."

How would they proceed? Will they reject this fully qualified man as a United States Senator because the governor filling the vacancy, unlike all other citizens, is judged guilty as charged without the right to a trial by a jury of his peers. Gov. Blagojevich has been charged, not convicted. Is it still possible to say this: the governor is innocent until proven guilty.

How does it look when the Senate throws away the presumption of innocence by threatening to obstruct a legal appointment based on the presumed guilt of the governor making the appointment?

Senators Must Obey the Laws, Too

Why didn't just one Senator stand up and point out that the appointment of Roland Burris was made by a sitting governor according to the laws of the State of Illinois, as the Constitution provides?

Will just one Senator on the Republican side take Sen. Cornyn to task for his obstructionist threat regarding Al Franken?

Why are they so special that they don't have to follow the rules?

We're witnessing the beginning of the 111th Congress engaged in the wholesale disrespect of the law in favor of partisan bias. There is no regard for the law, no regard for process, and no indication of even the slightest degree of insight on the part of those [flouting] the laws. There isn't even one objection to the violation of process, rules, and law from any Senator.

The majority of citizens are subject to the laws as they stand. If you steal an iPod, that's a felony in most states. You'll do some time if you can't afford an attorney. If the felony stands, you'll lose your right to vote in many states. In all instances, a felony places huge barriers to gainful employment, including a career in any of the professions.

Yet when it comes time to obey the Constitution that they're obliged to honor and protect, what do the Senators do? They allow their personal bias and political interests to trump the Constitution without any noticeable objection from the legislative body.

This type of disregard for the law by lawmakers is not only unacceptable; it impedes citizens from implementing their own "bailouts" and "recovery" programs by denying them access and positive influence on the government in this critical period of our history.

Memo to Congress: Try following your own rules, precedents, and, most importantly, the Constitution of the United States. The laws and rules that Congress should follow are fairly straightforward and the underlying principles are clear—respond to the will of the people and respect their right to representation.

The Seventeenth Amendment Did Not Go Far Enough

Jennifer Rubin

Writing for Commentary *magazine's blog* Contentions *on December 17, 2008, journalist and attorney Jennifer Rubin argues that the Seventeenth Amendment did not, perhaps, go far enough. It left to the states the right to follow their own procedures for choosing replacements for senators who left office for whatever reason, and most states allowed governors to name replacements rather than hold special elections. To Rubin's mind this created great openings for corruption and even nepotism.*

The question of senatorial replacements was important following the national elections of November 2008. Senators Barack Obama of Illinois and Joe Biden of Delaware had just been elected president and vice president, respectively, while Obama's cabinet members would later include Hillary Rodham Clinton and Ken Salazar, senators from New York and Colorado, respectively. Rubin points out that the replacement of Obama was tainted by the alleged criminal behavior of Illinois governor Rod Blagojevich. Meanwhile, the replacements of Biden and Salazar might well be relatives of the two former senators while, as of December 2008, the frontrunner to replace Clinton was Caroline Kennedy, the daughter of former President John F. Kennedy and niece of Senator Edward Kennedy of Massachusetts. Caroline Kennedy had never held public office. According to Rubin, special elections were far preferable to such "anointing" of senatorial replacements.

As it turned out, Blagojevich appointed Roland Burris to replace Obama while Delaware governor Ruth Ann Miner indeed appointed Joe Biden's chief of staff, Ted Kaufman, to Biden's Senate seat. In Colorado, Michael Bennett ultimately took

Jennifer Rubin, "Who Knew the 17th Amendment Was Such a Good Idea?" *Commentary Magazine*, December 17, 2008. Reproduced by permission.

Salazar's seat, while in New York, Caroline Kennedy ended weeks of speculation in January 2009 by announcing she would not seek to replace Clinton. The New York seat was filled instead by Kirsten Gillibrand.

The Seventeenth Amendment, providing for the direct election of senators, was ratified almost a hundred years ago. Since then, it's had its ups and downs. For every Everett Dirksen, [respected Illinois senator from 1951 to 1965,] there's been a Ted Stevens [Alaska senator from 1968 to 2009 accused of corruption]. But we generally have gotten along on the theory that these rather powerful people should be popularly elected.

Not so much this year [2008]. We have seats filled or to be filled by Governors in Delaware (by now Vice-President Joe Biden's staffer to keep the seat warm for Biden's son), New York (where the frontrunner is the princess who has everything [Caroline Kennedy], so why not a senate seat?), Illinois (if they can figure out how to hold out long enough to impeach Blago [Governor Rod Blagojevich] first), and now Colorado (the brother of the current senator [Ken Salazar] is the frontrunner—I kid you not). This isn't a good idea for *lots* of reasons. (I admit this against all self-interest since this is pure comedy and journalistic gold.)

Beholden Senators

Let's put aside the Blago/criminality element, well sort of. The appointment by a governor of a senator creates a relationship in which the latter is entirely beholden to the former, even more so than a normal senator would be to a governor of the same party. There need not be an explicit *quid pro quo* to realize that there's virtually nothing that appointee won't do for the governor—be it judges, policies, waivers of federal requirements, bailouts and the like. And because of the circumstances of the appointment the suspicion will always be, regardless of the merits, that the governor is pulling the strings.

A courtroom drawing depicts former Illinois governor Rod Blagojevich, his chief of staff John Harris, and prosecutor Reid Schar. Blagojevich was arrested and charged with federal corruption and has since been removed from office. © Verna Sadock/epa/Corbis.

Then there are the candidates themselves. With an appointment, there is no winnowing in primaries or vetting in elections. Whatever we don't know about them we won't find out until they are in office. Whatever faults they have will be sprung upon the voters only after they are sworn in. This is especially fraught with peril when the appointee is someone who never held elective office.

You only need look at the choices this year to know that this is cronyism at its worse. A Biden staffer holding out for Biden's son? You must be joking! The daughter of a president, sponsored by the uncle senator [Edward Kennedy of Massachusetts] whose greatest public contribution is carrying the torch of her troubled family? We owe George III [king of England during the American Revolution] an apology for all those royalty cracks, if this one slips through. Almost by definition these picks aren't the most meritorious; they are the most connected. They had to be to get the nod.

Republicans are certainly licking their chops at the chance to run in 2010 against the related and the anointed. The very circumstances of these individuals' elevation will raise many voters' ire.

So what to do? All the open seats should be filled by special election. And if the money is tight in states, that's one bailout of federal money I'd favor. Spending money on democratic elections seems about the best use of the taxpayers' money one can imagine. As we see, the alternative is an embarrassment.

States That Appoint Senate Replacements Should Hold Special Elections Instead

Jerry H. Goldfeder

In the following selection, attorney and legal scholar Jerry H. Goldfeder argues that special elections should be held in states like New York, where in 2008 a replacement had to be chosen for Senator Hillary Rodham Clinton, who had been named the new U.S. secretary of state. Goldfeder notes that New York, like forty-five other states, either permits or requires the governor to appoint a senatorial replacement rather than hold a special election. These replacements remain in their seats until the next election cycle. By contrast, replacements for members of the House of Representatives are always chosen by special election.

Goldfeder notes that the Seventeenth Amendment provides for governor-appointed replacements and that Wisconsin senator Russ Feingold was proposing a new amendment mandating special elections instead. But in the meantime, Goldfeder argues that individual states should exercise their option to mount special elections rather than settle for often-contentious gubernatorial appointments. Jerry H. Goldfeder is a special counsel at the New York law firm of Stroock & Stroock & Lavan and the author of Goldfeder's Modern Election Law.

No doubt the last time anyone thought about the exact wording of the presidential oath of office was on Nov. 22, 1963 when federal Judge Sara T. Hughes had to scramble for a copy of the U.S. Constitution to administer the oath to Lyndon B. Johnson aboard Air Force One. Of course, that was an unanticipated event, occurring only a little while after President John F. Kennedy was assassinated. [Current] Chief Justice John Roberts, on the other hand, prepared for his role and the task ahead [administering the oath of office to Barack Obama in January 2009]. Swearing in a president for the first time, I suppose, is enough to make anyone a little nervous, however, and as the whole world watched, he did not get it exactly right. And so, with an "abundance of caution," the oath was re-administered, or perhaps administered for the first time. We should, however, be thankful to the chief justice for reminding us of the actual text and the legal import of oaths.

It is also likely that most New York lawyers have not thought about the 17th Amendment to the Constitution since 1968, the year Senator Robert Kennedy was assassinated. This amendment requires direct election of U.S. Senators, and includes a provision for replacing senators when vacancies occur. Of course, the 17th Amendment is in the news because of the number of high-profile Senate vacancies this year [2008], the seats of President Barack Obama in Illinois; Secretary of State Hillary Rodham Clinton in New York; Vice President Joseph Biden in Delaware; and Secretary of the Interior Ken Salazar in Colorado.

The vacancy provision appears simple enough. A governor shall issue "writs of election to fill such vacancies," but "the legislature of any State may empower the executive thereof to make temporary appointments until the people fill the vacancies by election as the legislature may direct." This has been interpreted to mean that if a state has opted to allow for a temporary appointee, she may serve until an election is required pursuant to that jurisdiction's election code. In New York, in the circumstances of Ms. Clinton's vacancy, newly appointed Senator Kirsten Gillibrand does not face the voters until November 2010, almost two full years after assuming office.

This revelation may have come as a surprise to most voters, indeed, to most lawyers who do not specialize in the area. The news is especially startling after an election year in which so many people were actively engaged. And it certainly seems odd in light of the fact that when there is a vacancy in many other offices, there are special elections after a short period of time: the [New York] state Legislature, the [New York] city council and the [U.S.] House of Representatives, for example; though, I should add, not for New York State attorney general or comptroller.

It is curious that the U.S. Constitution requires immediate special elections for members of the House, but not the Senate. Thus, in 1968, when [New York] Governor [Nelson] Rockefeller appointed Charles Goodell to fill Senator Kennedy's seat, voters went to court to force an immediate election rather than allow him to serve as an appointed senator until the end of 1970. They obviously lost. In *Valenti v. Rockefeller*, a three-judge panel held that an "extended" appointment period was not unconstitutional, and, in particular, not contrary to the 17th Amendment. When there is a U.S. Senate seat vacancy in New York, voters must wait until the general election in the next even-numbered year. Three factors led to this result: the plain language of the 17th Amendment; the customary practice and laws of other states; and the substantial state interest in having a vote during a regularly scheduled election. Judge Marvin Frankel dissented, terming the majority's decision "an unprecedented extension of the 'temporary' appointive power." Nevertheless, the decision was affirmed without opinion by the U.S. Supreme Court.

New York is not alone in providing for appointments of replacement senators. A whopping 45 other states also permit appointment, allowing the replacement senator to serve until the next election. Twenty-two of these states have permissive appointment laws, where the governor is not required to name a replacement; the other 23 have mandatory appointment laws like New York. And, depending upon when the vacancy occurs, the appointee in almost three-quarters of these states does not have to face voters for as long as two years.

Moreover, some states have unique or special peculiarities. For example, in Louisiana the governor's appointment may serve out the unexpired term only if a year or less remains on the term; in Iowa and Texas the governor makes an appointment only if the vacancy occurs or will occur while Congress is in session. Had [Republican presidential candidate and Arizona senator] John McCain won the presidential election, the Governor of Arizona would have appointed his replacement. But that state has its own wrinkle. The temporary appointee must be from the same political party as the outgoing senator. Were this to have occurred, Democratic Governor Janet Napolitano would have been required to choose a Republican. Three other states follow the same practice: Hawaii, Utah and Wyoming. Interestingly, in New Hampshire, which does not require a governor to appoint a replacement from the same party as the outgoing senator, the Democratic governor was all set to replace Republican Senator Judd Gregg with another Republican when Gregg seemed headed to the Commerce Department.

Only four states mandate a special election to fill a vacancy in the U.S. Senate. Massachusetts, Oklahoma, Oregon and Wisconsin require elections, and do not provide for appointments. Oklahoma's statute is a bit quirky, though: it does not apply if the vacancy occurs after March 1 of the last year of the term. In that situation, the candidate elected at the general election is appointed by the governor for the remainder of the unexpired term; that law leaves Oklahomans without a senator for up to nine months.

And then there is Alaska. After former Governor Frank Murkowski appointed his daughter to the very Senate seat he himself had vacated, the people of Alaska voted in a referendum to join the small club of states that require immediate

Senator Russell Feingold asserts that the U.S. Constitution should require states to hold special elections to fill Senate vacancies. Getty Images.

special elections; however, Alaska also has a statute that provides for an interim appointment pending the special election.

Senator Russ Feingold (D-Wisc.) is proposing to amend the U.S. Constitution to require all states to conduct special elections to fill Senate vacancies. Of course, the amendment process is long and arduous. Therefore, unless and until such an amendment passes, New York State retains the option to change its own law. It should.

A Respected Senator Plans Ahead

Fredreka Schouten and Kathy Kiely

Senator Edward M. Kennedy, the younger brother of assassinated president John F. Kennedy, served the state of Massachusetts in the U.S. Senate from 1962 to 2009, making him one of the institution's longest-serving and most respected members. He was diagnosed with brain cancer in May 2008. In the following selection, USA Today *writers Fredreka Schouten and Kathy Kiely report on a request Kennedy made to the Massachusetts state government in the summer of 2009, just days before his death. He asked the state to devise a rapid procedure for replacing him.*

Massachusetts was one of the few states to not automatically allow its governor to appoint senatorial replacements, requiring instead a special election within five months. The state's dominant Democratic Party had instituted the requirement in 2004, hoping to deny then governor Mitt Romney, a Republican, the ability to appoint a replacement in the event that John Kerry, the state's other senator, was elected president. Kennedy's request asked the governor and legislature of Massachusetts to act quickly to devise new procedures and allow the governor to appoint at least a temporary replacement.

Senator Kennedy passed away on August 25, 2009. By late September both the Massachusetts House of Representatives and Senate had approved a measure permitting Governor Deval Patrick to appoint a temporary replacement, thus making sure the state maintained its full complement of two senators. A special election was scheduled for January 2010 to choose a permanent replacement for Kennedy.

An ailing Sen. Edward Kennedy is urging Massachusetts' political leaders to change state law to assure his swift replacement if he has to surrender his seat.

Gov. Deval Patrick and the state's top Democratic legislative leaders did not indicate whether they would act on Kennedy's request. The legislature, currently in informal session until early September [2009], would have to hold a public hearing and schedule a formal vote, said Secretary of State William Galvin, a Democrat who oversees elections.

"They are not going to entertain it very quickly," he said.

Revelation of the letter came on the heels of an announcement that the publication date of Kennedy's memoirs, originally set for early October, has been moved up to next month [September].

Aides downplayed any speculation that the moves signalled a worsening of the senator's health. As Massachusetts politicians debated the senator's suggestion in the media, Kennedy was enjoying an afternoon on his sailboat, according to Anthony Coley, a spokesman in the senator's Washington office.

Coley said Kennedy has been sailing "almost every day" this summer.

The letter is dated July 2 but Kennedy did not send it to Patrick until earlier this week [of August 20], Coley said. He said the delay was because the senator was "preoccupied" with the final illness of his sister, Eunice Shriver. She died Aug. 11.

Norman Ornstein, a veteran Congress-watcher with the American Enterprise Institute, said that Kennedy's letter is a sign that the canny lawmaker is continuing to count votes— and is worried his party might come up short on controversial measures such as the president's proposals for overhauling health care and addressing climate change.

"It's his realization that he may not be around when all these critical votes take place," said Ornstein. "It's going to be very close."

Scott Brown, a Republican, defeated his Democrat opponent in a 2010 U.S. Senate special election to serve out the remainder of the term of Senator Ted Kennedy, who died in 2009. AP Images.

Massachusetts is one of about six states that does not allow the governor to fill a Senate vacancy, says Ornstein. A senior adviser to the bipartisan Continuity of Government Commission—co-chaired by former senators Alan Simpson, a Wyoming Republican, and David Pryor, an Arkansas Democrat—Ornstein is a leading proponent for allowing temporary appointments to vacant congressional seats.

Ornstein began pushing Congress to consider ways to reconstitute itself after the 9/11 terror attacks [in 2001]. If replacement lawmakers can't be appointed immediately, the detonation of a weapon of mass destruction in Washington could leave the nation without a working Congress for months, Ornstein said. "That means martial law," he added.

Currently, Massachusetts law requires a special-election within five months to fill any vacancy and does not grant Patrick the power to fill the seat in the interim. In a letter to

Patrick, Senate President Therese Murray and House Speaker Robert DeLeo, Kennedy said it was crucial for state residents to have "two votes in the Senate during the approximately five months between a vacancy and an election."

Kennedy also asked state leaders to require that anyone appointed to the seat agree not to compete in the special election.

Kennedy's request was first reported by *The Boston Globe*.

Kennedy, 77, was diagnosed with brain cancer in May 2008 and has been out of Washington and the public view for months—even as Congress tackles a health-care overhaul that the Democrat has called the "cause of his life." He did not attend a public funeral service for his sister, Eunice Kennedy Shriver.

Passage of the health-care initiative could rest on a handful of Senate votes, and Kennedy's allies, such as Ron Pollack of Families USA, say the senator's move reflects his commitment to making the overhaul law.

"If, unfortunately, he does not live to see the key vote in the Senate," Pollack said, "he wants to make sure that his succession is handled in such a way that his legacy is truly achieved."

Kennedy's letter, dated July 2, was sent to political leaders this week. He does not address his cancer, which has required surgery, chemotherapy and radiation.

"For almost 47 years, I have had the privilege of representing the people of Massachusetts in the United States Senate," Kennedy wrote. He said serving "has been—and still is—the greatest honor of my public life."

Democrats control both chambers of the Massachusetts legislature by wide margins, but would face resistance to Kennedy's proposal from the GOP ranks, said Senate Minority Leader Richard Tisei, the top Republican in the state Senate.

The Democratic-controlled legislature changed the state's succession law in 2004, denying then-governor Mitt Romney, a Republican, the ability to fill a Senate vacancy as Democratic Sen. John Kerry competed for the White House.

"I feel terrible for Sen. Kennedy," Tisei said. But he said it would be "very hard for the Democratic majority to change the law when they so passionately advocated" to alter it in 2004. "We shouldn't be changing the laws based on personal circumstances."

Murray and DeLeo, the legislature's top Democrats, issued a joint statement saying they hoped Kennedy would "continue to be a voice for the people of Massachusetts as long as he is able." [Although Governor Patrick appointed a Democrat, Paul Kirk, as Kennedy's replacement, Massachusetts voters chose Republican Scott Brown in the January 2010 special election to take his seat.]

Appendix

Appendix

The Amendments to the U.S. Constitution

Amendment I: Freedom of Religion, Speech, Press, Petition, and
                  Assembly (ratified 1791)

Amendment II: Right to Bear Arms (ratified 1791)

Amendment III: Quartering of Soldiers (ratified 1791)

Amendment IV: Freedom from Unfair Search and Seizures
                  (ratified 1791)

Amendment V: Right to Due Process (ratified 1791)

Amendment VI: Rights of the Accused (ratified 1791)

Amendment VII: Right to Trial by Jury (ratified 1791)

Amendment VIII: Freedom from Cruel and Unusual Punishment
                  (ratified 1791)

Amendment IX: Construction of the Constitution (ratified 1791)

Amendment X: Powers of the States and People (ratified 1791)

Amendment XI: Judicial Limits (ratified 1795)

Amendment XII: Presidential Election Process (ratified 1804)

Amendment XIII: Abolishing Slavery (ratified 1865)

Amendment XIV: Equal Protection, Due Process, Citizenship for All
                  (ratified 1868)

The Amendments to the U.S. Constitution

Amendment XV: Race and the Right to Vote (ratified 1870)
Amendment XVI: Allowing Federal Income Tax (ratified 1913)
Amendment XVII: Establishing Election to the U.S. Senate
                   (ratified 1913)
Amendment XVIII: Prohibition (ratified 1919)
Amendment XIX: Granting Women the Right to Vote (ratified 1920)
Amendment XX: Establishing Term Commencement for Congress
                   and the President (ratified 1933)
Amendment XXI: Repeal of Prohibition (ratified 1933)
Amendment XXII: Establishing Term Limits for U.S. President
                   (ratified 1951)
Amendment XXIII: Allowing Washington, D.C., Representation in the
                   Electoral College (ratified 1961)
Amendment XXIV: Prohibition of the Poll Tax (ratified 1964)
Amendment XXV: Presidential Disability and Succession
                   (ratified 1967)
Amendment XXVI: Lowering the Voting Age (ratified 1971)
Amendment XXVII: Limiting Congressional Pay Increases
                   (ratified 1992)

For Further Research

Books

Akhil Reed Amar, *America's Constitution: A Biography*. New York: Random House, 2005.

Robert C. Byrd, *The Senate, 1789–1989: Addresses on the History of the United States Senate*. Washington, DC: Government Printing Office, 1991.

Brett Flehinger, *The 1912 Election and the Power of Progressivism: A History with Documents*. Boston: Bedford/St. Martin's, 2003.

Lewis L. Gould, *The Most Exclusive Club: A History of the Modern United States Senate*. New York: Basic Books, 2005.

———, *Reform and Regulation: American Politics from Roosevelt to Wilson*. New York: Knopf, 1986.

Robert Harrison, *Congress, Progressive Reform, and the New American State*. New York: Cambridge University Press, 2004.

George H. Haynes, *The Senate of the United States: Its History and Practice*. Boston: Houghton Mifflin, 1938.

C.H. Hoebeke, *The Road to Mass Democracy: Original Intent and the Seventeenth Amendment*. New Brunswick, NJ: Transaction, 1995.

Ralph Rossum, *Federalism, The Supreme Court, and the Seventeenth Amendment: The Irony of Constitutional Democracy*. Lanham, MD: Lexington Books, 2001.

David Sarasohn, *The Party of Reform: Democrats in the Progressive Era*. Jackson: University Press of Mississippi, 1989.

Joel Arthur Tarr, *A Study in Boss Politics: William Lorimer of Chicago*. Urbana: University of Illinois Press, 1971.

Periodicals

Jay S. Bybee, "Ulysses at the Mast: Democracy, Federalism, and the Siren's Song of the Seventeenth Amendment," *Northwestern University Law Review*, vol. 91, 1997.

Larry J. Easterling, "Senator Joseph L. Bristow and the Seventeenth Amendment," *Kansas Historical Quarterly*, vol. 41, 1975.

C.H. Hoebeke, "Democratizing the Constitution: The Failure of the Seventeenth Amendment," *Humanitas*, vol. 9, no. 2, 1996.

Richard L. McCormick, "The Discovery That Business Corrupts Politics: A Reappraisal of the Origins of Progressivism," *American Historical Review*, vol. 86, 1981.

John B. Wiseman, "Racism in Democratic Politics, 1904–1912," *Mid-America*, vol. 51, 1968.

Internet Sources

Bruce Bartlett, "Repeal the 17th Amendment," *National Review Online*, May 12, 2004. www.nationalreview.com.

James Boyce, "How the 17th Amendment Was Supposed to Save Us from Being Blago'd," *The Huffington Post*, December 29, 2008. www.huffingtonpost.com.

Brian Dickerson, "A Way to Restore the People's Senate," *Detroit Free Press*, August 27, 2009. www.freep.com.

Thomas J. DiLorenzo, "Repeal the 17th Amendment," LewRockwell.com, May 17, 2005. www.lewrockwell.com.

Michael Dorf, "Senator Kirk and the Constitutionality of Expedient Law Switching," Dorfonlaw.org, September 25, 2009. www.dorfonlaw.org.

Michael Frost, "Maryland Never Ratified the Seventeenth Amendment to U.S. Constitution," *Southern Maryland Online*, February 24, 2009. http://somd.com.

Katha Pollitt, "Wise Words on the 17th Amendment," *The Nation*, January 22, 2009. www.thenation.com.

Chad Rubel, "No Constitutional Amendment Necessary: People Already Have Power to Make Senate Replacement Changes," Buzzflash, January 28, 2009. http://blog .buzzflash.com.

Michael Streich, "Progressive Era Reforms and the 17th Amendment," Suite101.com, December 7, 2008. http:// modern-us-history.suite101.com.

John W. Truslow III, "Senate Vacancies Raise Questions of Framers' Intentions," *Roll Call*, October 5, 2009. www.rollcall.com.

Web Sites

The Constitution Society, www.constitution.org. An elaborate Web site devoted to the society's understanding of constitutional principles. It maintains links to original documents and images as well as to a wide variety of constitutional controversies.

U.S. Constitution Online, www.usconstitution.net/const.html. This Web site provides the full Constitution with amendments. It features commentary and explanations of all the amendments.

The U.S. Senate, www.senate.gov. The official Web site of the U.S. Senate. While focusing on the contemporary Senate, it also features links to historical topics and to reference materials.

Index